DICK JOHNSON

WORKING FOR DEMOCRACY

Working for Democracy

AMERICAN WORKERS FROM THE REVOLUTION
TO THE PRESENT

Edited by Paul Buhle and Alan Dawley

Foreword by Herbert G. Gutman

University of Illinois Press   *Urbana and Chicago*

This book is printed on acid-free paper.

Library of Congress Cataloging in Publication Data

Main entry under title:

Working for democracy.

   Bibliography: p.
   1. Labor and laboring classes—United States—
History—Addresses, essays, lectures. 2. Labor supply—
United States—History—Addresses, essays, lectures.
3. Trade-unions—United States—History—Addresses,
essays, lectures. I. Buhle, Paul, 1944-
II. Dawley, Alan, 1943-
HD8066.W67   1985   331'.0973   85-5845
ISBN 0-252-01220-8 (cloth; alk. paper)
ISBN 0-252-01221-6 (paper; alk. paper)

To the memory of
Barbara Mayer Wertheimer
1925–1983

Contents

Foreword

The history of American society is the history of inequality of all kinds: economic, sexual, and racial. But it is much more than that. It is also the history of how poor men and women have won their democratic rights, how they have organized and used their power to try to expand their rights and to combat their unequal status.

This brief volume examining working people's responses to inequality is welcome in the 1980s for many reasons. It is most important because we live at a time when influential and powerful Americans, the president prominent among them, attack the concept of equality and insist that inequality is essential to progress. Second, it can help working people themselves to address the questions raised by such leaders. Written for labor studies, adult education, and undergraduate courses, as well as for the general public, the book provides the basis for a discussion that can make history come to life as rehearsal for the present.

This book contains fourteen short chapters by well-known historians of the American working class, American women, Afro-Americans, or anti-capitalist movements. The chapters have a particular and very useful focus. They emphasize how working people have used their power—in the workplace, the polling booth, and the streets—to alter their unequal condition. They highlight the recurrent democratic and collective struggles by working men and women and by white and black workers either to improve the material circumstances of wage earners and their families, or to alter the structure of inequality bred by a changing capitalist economy, or sometimes both. They start in the era of the American Revolution, when hardly any free Americans worked for wages; they end in the era of Jimmy Carter and Ronald Reagan, a time of economic stagnation and capitalist crisis. They stretch over two full centuries, describing and analyzing some of the most important moments in our history.

The basic fact in workers' lives is their dependence on others for the means to live. That is true regardless of where they live: in the changing South, the booming Sun Belt, or the declining northeastern and midwestern industrial towns and cities. It is true whether they belong to trade unions or other popular protective associations, and it is true no matter what kind of work they do. They may labor in mechanized factories, in the mines, in transport, or in building maintenance. They may work in fast food shops and other retail enterprises, in offices and schools, in hospitals and firehouses. Their employers can be large multinational corporations, small firms, or local, state, and federal governments. They differ from one another according to sex, race, age, education, places of birth and residence, as well as by the nature of their work. But all share a common unequal condition.

Dependence upon others for the means to live shapes workers' experiences and outlook in distinctive ways. Alexander Hamilton, one of this nation's founders and most articulate political thinkers, realized this: "Give a man power over my subsistence," he warned two centuries ago, "and he has a right to my whole moral body." Hamilton's observation applies as fully to the dominance of men over women and whites over blacks as to the dominance of employers over wage workers. His statement also is a *historical* statement, its meaning changing over time. His observation was appropriate in the late eighteenth century and remains appropriate in the late twentieth, even though the society in which we live differs from that in which Hamilton lived.

Historical understanding explains those differences and teaches us that much that we assume as fixed and unchanging in our lives actually has a history. Planting and harvesting have a history. So does the family. Hemlines, dancing, and baseball have histories. So does diet. Presidential politics and foreign policy have a history. So does work. And so do wage labor and inequality, dependence and domination—and resistance to domination. Historical understanding teaches us to transform the seemingly fixed and eternal in our lives into things that can be changed. It teaches working people that the structures surrounding them have been made and remade, over and over. It teaches that we live in history.

The historical context changes over time, and so does the language of resistance. Two examples illustrate these changes. Philadelphia journeymen carpenters explained why they formed a trade union in 1791: "'Tis one of the invaluable privileges of our nature, that when we conceive ourselves aggrieved, there is an inherent right to complain.... Self-preservation has induced us to enter into an indissoluble union, in order to ward off the blows which are threatened us, by the insolent hand of pampered affluence:—We mean hereafter by a firm, independent mode of conduct to protect each other...." The Philadelphia carpenters had taken the ideas of their "betters" (men like Alexander Hamilton) and put them to a new use.

And hear this report of rural South Carolina blacks seeking ways to sustain schools in 1868. Cash was short. One urged that "rich and poor ... come forward at once and assist in support of the schools, each putting in according to his means." He advised that all "set aside a piece of land, work it fruitfully, and devote all its produce to the schools." Another spoke: "Uncle Liah ... said they were all poor, and each could do but little, but this was work for many. It may be as it was at Indian Hill, where the great burial-ground was raised by each Indian throwing just one handful of earth upon it each time he passed...." The South Carolina ex-slaves had learned not from their "betters," but from their native American neighbors.

The Philadelphia carpenters and South Carolina blacks lived

at different times, worked in different settings, and used language differently to reveal their collective discontent. Theirs were not isolated expressions. Resistance to inequality surfaced in popular movements again and again from the 1830s to the 1960s. These movements carry us from the demand for free education and land, to cooperatives and democratic socialism, to industrial unionism, and, recently, to civil rights and welfare rights.

Despite the civil rights and women's movements in our time, awareness of working people's past efforts to alter their unequal condition diminished after 1945. In part, that happened in the aftermath of the Great Boom of 1945–70, the longest sustained economic boom in the history of American capitalism. That quarter-century sanitized popular historical consciousness. But that moment has ended. Inequality as a political issue is being debated again in the 1980s. The essays in this volume remind us that the debate is not a new one; the political and economic context is very different, but not the debate itself. That is what working people will learn in reading and discussing *Working for Democracy*.

—Herbert G. Gutman

Preface

This book began as a newspaper series popularizing discoveries made by labor historians during the 1960s and 1970s. Most of the contributors, like both of us, have worked in and around the labor movement. There, we discovered, the need for a new treatment of workers' history has never been greater. Retelling the old stories about the formation of unions and recalling the heroes of yesteryear's strikes no longer have the familiar heart-warming effect. Changes in the location and nature of production and changes in the workforce threaten to wipe out any sense of continuity. We asked ourselves how our understanding of the past had altered since the "institutional" histories of individual unions and labor leaders had been written. Because civil rights campaigns had brought the labor movement to question its own limitations, race would have to be seen in a new way. Because of the women's movement, so would gender. Recent shifts in voting patterns among white male workers in particular raised troubling questions about Labor's political loyalties. Current problems underlined the necessity for a wider historical reconsideration. The labor movement could no longer be calculated as the sum of union members, hours lost to industry in strikes, and the "labor vote" at elections. Labor organizations had always existed within a society whose fate its ranks shared, for good and ill. Labor history had to become a part of social history.

The task presents formidable problems, but a new generation of scholar-activists has begun to work on a collective solution,

engaging unionists and the public at large in a far-reaching dia-
logue about labor's heritage. Documentary films such as *Harlan
County, Union Maids,* and *Rosie the Riveter* have received an
enthusiastic response not only in unions halls but also on college
campuses, in churches, among women's organizations, and in
living rooms where public television reaches millions. Labor
troubadours have sprung up by the dozens, singing contemporary and historical tunes before wide-ranging audiences.
Labor history societies in increasing numbers have collected
union records, led walking tours, prepared exhibits and slide
shows for schools and libraries, arranged banquets and Labor
Day parades. Union members have joined with religious and
minority leaders in like-minded community projects to reclaim
the local past. An exciting "amateur" literature, from pictorial
histories to collections of labor poetry and humor, has found
a ready audience. Labor studies courses have become a recognized branch of colleges and of the labor movement itself. More
than a few younger local labor leaders take pride in their own
historical knowledge, their collections of memorabilia, their
sense of tradition connected with the struggles of the present. A
number of national publications (including the weekly newspaper
In These Times, in which most of these essays first appeared, and
the monthly *Labor Notes*) have begun to report regularly on the
trends and themselves to bridge the gap between scholarship and
popular movements.

We have only begun, and, in these ill times for labor, we have
far to go. A book such as this provides only one element for
developing understanding and rigorous education. One cannot
yet gauge the significance of the new labor history in an era of
declining union memberships, deserted industrial valleys, and
an adversarial government attitude toward labor organization.
Probably labor education has as much prospect as the tradition
of solidarity now facing the brave new world of video display
terminals and robotic assembly lines. Time will tell. The "lessons"
of history are no longer simple—if they ever were.

Nor do we claim a comprehensive view here, for no short book can provide that. Mexican-American labor in particular, and Latin American-originated labor in general, demand a closer exmaination; the history of women's labor has been inadequately discussed. Relevant political movements of the left, the Communists in particular, have not been seriously taken up here. Neither have their counterparts on the right, racist and conservative-religious entities. We leave such work to the future, confident that we have succeeded in making some of the new historical knowledge available to those who can use it best.

WORKING FOR DEMOCRACY

Portion of silk banner carried by the Society of Pewterers of New York City in the federal procession, July 23, 1788, by which New York celebrated ratification of the Constitution. Courtesty of New-York Historical Society, New York City.

Revolutionary Mechanics

Alfred F. Young

Where does the history of American labor begin? What are the roots of radicalism among American workers? For too many Americans there is no labor history until the rise of the factory, no radicalism until modern European ideas made their way to the United States.

In the nineteenth century many working people and radicals thought otherwise. They recognized a time when American workers helped make a revolution—the American Revolution—and bent the institutions of government toward democracy.

Countless unions, labor parties, and reform groups couched their grievances in the language of the Declaration of Independence. In 1860, when the shoemakers of Lynn, Massachusetts, conducted the biggest strike up to the Civil War, they began it on George Washington's birthday and placed the American flag at the head of their parade.

In 1876, on the centennial celebration of the Revolution, Wendell Phillips—the great abolitionist who after the Civil War went on to believe in "the overthrow of the whole profit-making system"—expressed the other side of this same theme: "It was the mechanics of Boston that threw the tea into the docks; it was the mechanics of Boston that held up the hands of Sam Adams; it was the mechanics of Boston, Paul Revere among them, that made the Green Dragon [Tavern] immortal.... The men who carried us through the Revolution were the mechanics of Boston."

What did Wendell Phillips and the Lynn shoemakers know

1

about the Revolution that would be almost totally lost by the time of the Bicentennial in 1976?

An early American mechanic was a skilled craftsman. Sometimes he was called a tradesman—a man with a trade. He might be a master, a journeyman, or an apprentice. On the eve of the Revolution most mechanics lived in the major cities, such as Philadelphia, the largest, with a population of 35,000; New York with 20,000; Boston with 16,000, Newport or Charleston. In a country with 2 million whites and 500,000 slaves, about 100,000 people lived in the large cities, where from one-half to two-thirds of the adult males were in the mechanic classes. Most were of British origin; a sprinkling were from northern and western Europe; all but a handful were Protestant.

The cities were seaports and they were growing, which meant that large numbers of mechanics were in the maritime trades (shipyards, ropewalks, and sailcloth lofts) or in the building trades. Other mechanics produced goods for consumers (blacksmiths, silversmiths, cabinet makers, tailors and shoemakers), often in competition with manufactures imported from Britain. And there was a mixed group in the service trades: "the butcher, the baker, the candlestick maker."

A typical master mechanic owned his own shop, employing perhaps a journeyman and invariably a number of apprentices aged fourteen to twenty-one. A large-scale factory was a rarity; in the cities a shipyard with one or two dozen men or a ropewalk with ten was big. Full-fledged wage workers were numerous mostly in trades like these that required large capital investments. In many trades, apprentices who received room and board outnumbered journeymen.

Outside the skilled system there were large numbers of semiskilled workers: merchant seamen, cartmen, stevedores, and common laborers. At the very bottom were slaves, some skilled, most household servants, a small and declining proportion of all workers—at least in the northern cities. Women often assisted their husbands in the skilled trades; occasionally one took over her husband's shop on his death. Otherwise, they were in "women's" work, making lace or washing clothes, or were petty shopkeepers or keepers of grog shops.

Among mechanics a small minority were successful, well-to-do men; the printer Benjamin Franklin, for example, or the silver-smith Paul Revere. At the bottom were a growing number of propertyless men and women in the "lower" trades who knew the inside of the poorhouse. And precariously perched between were a large number of "middling" artisans who suffered hard times in seasonal unemployment or frequent trade dislocations and knew the inside of the debtors' prison.

Wealthy merchants stood at the top of the cities—export-import wholesalers who owned ships and warehouses. Whatever their condition, the status of mechanics was low. Even masters in the "higher" trades were not quite respectable in the eyes of "gentlemen" who put "Esq." after their names. And the "mechanic arts" were considered inferior to the "liberal arts."

A mechanic usually aspired to be "a man for himself." Some desired to rise up out of their trade, but most would probably have agreed with the "tanners, curriers and cord-wainers [shoe-makers]" of Philadelphia when they wrote in a petition, "the far greater number of us have been contented to live decently without acquiring wealth." "Our professions," they explained, "rendered us useful and necessary members of the community, proud of that rank, we aspired no higher." The virtues Benjamin Franklin preached in his almanacs—hard work, sobriety, and thrift—were popular and a source of pride among mechanics.

As measured by late definitions, there was no "labor movement" in the colonies. Yet there were long traditions of collective activity. It was common for artisans in a single trade in a city to join together on a temporary basis without establishing formal organizations: to set prices (the building trades); to cope with city rulers over mercantile regulations (bakers); to petition colonial assemblies for aid or relief. Self-generated activity among journeymen was far less frequent and strikes were unusual.

On the other hand, there was a thick web of custom by which

skilled workers set the pace on the job and defined what went on in the workshop. And in their communities mechanics shared equally strong traditions of collective action in crowds—the "better sort" would say "mobs"—of grain riots or market riots to enforce a just price, or riots against impressment into the British navy among sailors and dockworkers.

Before the Revolution, politics was generally a contest among elites. Most masters were qualified to vote, either in town meetings in New England or elsewhere for assembly elections. A lesser number usually were qualified to vote for city officials. Journeymen and laborers were all but disfranchised. When political contests heated up, gentlemen would appeal to mechanics, but "Shoemaker, stick to thy last" was their motto. Mechanics were not accustomed to meeting on their own for political purposes or to putting forth mechanic candidates. All this would change in the Revolution.

POLITICAL RESISTANCE

From 1765 to 1776 mechanics became active in the resistance to Britain. First, whatever affected the rights of colonists to retain self-government, like the parliamentary imposition of taxes, also affected them. In Philadelphia in 1773, "A Mechanic" argued that the Tea Act was oppressive, "whether we have property of our own, or not." A principle was at stake: "whether our property, and the dear earned fruits of our own labour are at our own disposal."

Second, some British actions affected workers directly. For merchant seamen, impressment was a continuing threat. British troops in Boston and New York were an abrasive presence, especially to journeymen with whom they competed for off-duty jobs.

Third, manufacturing became an issue. "It is sincerely to be lamented," wrote a Pennsylvanian, "that the mechanic arts and manufactures cannot be encouraged by our legislature ... but it happens somehow that our Mother County apprehends she has a right to manufacture every article we consume, except Bread and Meat." As patriots adopted the tactic of non-importation of British goods, the corollary, "Buy American," aroused a vision of the potential for American manufactures.

The range of political activity by mechanics was large and creative. Crowd action was the most spectacular. It was directed against royal officials to prevent the enforcement of new laws against informers who caused the arrest of colonials; against merchants who violated the boycott of British imports; against occupying troops. Crowds that tarred and feathered customs informers, or confronted soldiers, were usually workingmen's crowds.

Distinct committees of mechanics were a feature of New York and Philadelphia. They called meetings of "mechanics, tradesmen and manufacturers," passed resolutions, met with merchants' committees, chose delegates for joint committees, and ran mechanics for office. As resistance intensified, mechanics' militia companies often took the political initiative. In Philadelphia, the Committee of Privates, speaking for poor artisans and journeymen, became the backbone of the radicals, debating politics in actions reminiscent of Oliver Cromwell's army a century before.

In this wide range of activity mechanics responded to leaders of different sorts; to middle-class men popularly known as the Sons of Liberty, like Samuel Adams; to wealthy merchants who proved their patriotism, like John Hancock; and to men who emerged from the mechanic classes.

Mechanics were often divided, but as the political crisis deepened they tended to coalesce. There was a smaller proportion of Tories among them than among any other urban class. Within the patriot coalition, the strength of mechanics was related to the degree of patriotism among the merchants. In Philadelphia, where the wealthy abdicated or hung back in neutralism, mechanics rushed into the vacuum. In Boston, where the merchant class as a whole was patriotic and the popular leaders skillful, there were no separate mechanic committees and a low level of mechanic consciousness. New York was somewhere in between.

In the period of political resistance to Britain from 1765 to 1774, the seaboard cities—all capital cities and centers of impe-

rial power—were important out of proportion to their popula-
tions. Within the cities, mechanics and laborers in effect nullified
the Stamp Act, provided the physical coercion to enforce the
boycotts, took the lead in direct action against British troops,
provided the muscle for the Tea Parties, and effectively isolated
the Loyalists.

From 1774 to 1776, when resistance turned to rebellion,
mechanics were crucial. The first Continental Congress met in
Carpenters' Hall after it was denied the official state house by
Philadelphia conservatives. In 1776 *Common Sense,* written by
Thomas Paine, an English artisan attuned to Philadelphia's artisans, crystallized the sentiment for independence as opposed to
reconciliation. The most widely distributed pamphlet in eighteenth-
century America, *Common Sense* was written in the plain language of the common people and appealed to and reflected their
desire for a voice in government no less than their desire for
independence. Mechanics and farmers thus exerted the pressure
from below that moved reluctant rebels toward independence.

ARTISAN REPUBLICANISM

There was a progression in mechanic experience. As men participated in one crowd action after another, as crowds became
meetings, as meetings formed committees, as committees elected
candidates, mechanics recognized their capacity to shape events.

Every effort to put down mechanics only heightened their political consciousness. In Philadelphia, when mechanics put up
their own candidates and conservatives questioned the capacity
of "leather aprons" to govern, the reply was indignant: "Do not
mechanics and farmers constitute 99 out of 100 of the people of
America? ... Is not one-half the property of the city of Philadelphia owned by men who wear leather aprons?"

In Charleston, when an Anglican minister derided "every
silly clown and illiterate mechanic" for presuming to censure
their rulers, the local newspaper denounced him for this affront
"to the honest and industrious mechanic"; his congregation

(with a large number of mechanics) dismissed him, and a Rhode Island correspondent exclaimed: "All such divines should be taught to know that mechanics and country clowns (infamously so called) are the real and absolute masters of kings, lords, commons and priests, (though with shame be it spoken) they too often suffer their servants to get upon their backs and ride them most barbarously."

Mechanics asked for a political voice, not for control. They moved quickly toward demanding representation. Where the political system thwarted them, they asked for reforms, such as a secret ballot to eliminate voice voting. As independence loomed, they demanded a voice in the making of the new state constitutions; in New York a committee of mechanics claimed "a birthright" to accept or reject a constitution drafted by others; in Philadelphia they wanted a direct voice via "men of like passion and interests with ourselves." Where the political system accommodated them, as did the Boston town meeting, they made no demands for change.

In the states with big cities, the greater the mechanic influence and mechanic consciousness, the more democratic the constitution. Pennsylvania was the most radically democratic, Massachusetts and South Carolina the least, New York somewhere in between. The Pennsylvania constitution came closest to a democratic ideal: a one-house legislature, annual elections, nearly-universal male suffrage open to all who served in the militia, public office without property qualifications, rotation in office, a provision for public education.

Whatever the new institutions, there was increased mechanic participation in the political process. In the 1780s and 1790s more mechanics voted, more mechanic committees endorsed candidates, and more mechanics ran for and were elected to office.

Mechanics came out of seven years of war with a heightened sense of their importance as citizens. They were proud of what they had helped create. They demanded equal rights, and respect for their opinions and interests. They were suspicious of men of great wealth. They were not hostile to merchants as a class, or to commerce or property, but they distrusted "purse proud aristo-crats" or "great and overgrown rich men" who did not respect their rights.

Mechanics expressed pride in themselves as the producers of the wealth of society. The New York society's certificate por-trayed a carpenter at his lathe, a housewright putting up a build-ing, shipwrights in the yards, a smith at his forge, and a farmer at his plow. The central symbol, repeated in Charleston and Providence, was the raised muscular arm of a workman, his fist clenched around a sledgehammer. The motto was "By Hammer and Hand All Arts Do Stand," in Charleston varied to "Industry Produceth All Wealth." It was a proud assertion that the "mechanic and useful arts" were the basis of all wealth.

Mechanics also developed a national economic program: sup-port for American commerce, which would sustain the maritime trades, and the encouragement of American manufactures. From the mid-1780s mechanics in the major cities demanded a stronger national government to protect them from the ruinous renewal of British competition in shipping and imports.

With a political outlook such as this, mechanics could enter into a coalition with other "interests." In 1787–88 they saw in the new federal Constitution, drafted by middle-of-the-road con-servatives, the fulfillment of many of their aspirations for the Revolution. They showed this in the parades in celebration of ratification—the first labor parades in American history. In every major American city, mechanics marched by the thousands with other citizens.

This, then, was artisan republicanism: a conviction that me-chanics were citizens entitled to equal rights and to an equal voice in their government, a pride of craft, and a pride in labor as the source of wealth. It was based on the assumption that it was their Revolution, their war, their nation.

The mechanics passed on these traditions. The Fourth of July began, as early as the 1790s, as a holiday celebrated by mechan-ics. By the 1830s the new unions and labor parties treated the Fourth of July as a day to renew "the Spirit of '76."

As the economy changed and journeymen came into more conflict with masters, artisan republicanism came under severe strains. Masters, as the journeymen shoemakers said in Philadelphia in 1805, were "only the retailers of our labor . . . who in truth live upon the work of our hands." Masters were now "capitalists," not producers.

It was left to journeymen to push the ideals of artisan republicanism into new terrain. In 1809 the journeymen house carpenters of New York began their strike declaration with the words of the Declaration of Independence: "Among the unalienable rights of man are life, liberty and the pursuit of happiness." "By the social compact," they continued, "every *class* in society"—in itself a new phrase—"ought to be entitled to benefit *in proportion to its usefulness*"—a bold notion that made themselves, as the producers, more important than merchants or masters. They asked for compensation "not only for the current expenses of livelihood" but "for the formation of a fund" to support them in old age—what later generations would call social security.

These journeymen were drawing on the traditions of the American Revolution and of artisan republicanism. The labor movement in the nineteenth century would do the same as it confronted new enemies: monied aristocrats, slave power, and the robber barons.

SHIP
CARPENTERS
To Your Posts ! ! !

Moses H. Grinnell,
WILL NOT EMPLOY
Any Ship Carpenter, who Dares
TO AVOW HIS SUPPORT OF
THE HERO of NEW-ORLEANS.
Will ANY SHIP CAR-
PENTER, HAVING
THE SOUL OF A
FREEMAN,
Submit to such Aristocratic dictation ? You answer,
NO ! ! !
To the Polls then, Fellow Citizens, and shew that
Cornelius W. Lawrence,
**Who opposes the United States Bank, and supports
the PEOPLE, is the candidate of your choice.**

A political poster from the Jackson era. From Morris Bartel Schnapper, *American Labor: A Pictorial History* (Washington: Public Affairs Press, 1972).

Workingmen's Parties

Franklin Rosemont

The American labor movement was created by men and women conscious not only of the miserable conditions in which they were forced to live and work, but also of their power to change these conditions and to create a better world.

A half-century after the Revolution, it was not unusual for workers to labor seven days a week and twelve hours a day. For many families to make ends meet, even small children had to work the same long hours, but at even lower pay. Most workplaces and dwellings lacked adequate ventilation, sanitation, and rubbish removal. Medical care remained beyond the means of working-class families; mortality rates were high. Recurring epidemics decimated cities and towns. Even in good times workers' lives were hard; but there were also hard times, long periods of unemployment, inflation, and economic collapse brought on by financial panics.

To lessen their misery, sometimes in hopes of abolishing it, workers began to organize. There were clashes between wage earners and employers beginning in the 1780s, but these early collective efforts were designed to meet particular emergencies, after which the loose organizations disbanded. These precursors of trade unions also tended to restrict themselves to modest economic goals, such as resisting wage reductions. By the late 1820s workers increasingly began to recognize the need for permanent organizations, not only on the economic front, but also in politics.

The intervening years had seen great economic developments. In major eastern cities the Industrial Revolution eradicated the early American settlers' dreams of a peaceful pastoral republic. Thanks largely to British demand and to the sale of raw cotton produced by American slave labor, merchants remained all powerful. But native manufacturers had also begun their rapid ascent. As New England became a textile center, New York evolved into a distribution capital, linking industrialists with the burgeoning consumer market for clothes, shoes, and building materials. One venerable handicraft after another succumbed to the Age of Steam. The once-proud artisan found himself brutally shoved aside, his prestige greatly diminished, as he lost his livelihood to large firms, mechanization, and unskilled labor.

By common consent, the old ways were in crisis. Rising tensions and fears, as well as rising hopes and expectations, brought forth new religions and curious cults; some waited wild-eyed for an imminent day of doom, while others bristled with the certainty of a good time coming. Prophets and demagogues kindled the fires of the millennium anew and gave new life to ancient dreams of Heaven on Earth, the Garden of Eden restored, peace and plenty for all.

Amidst the growing dissatisfaction, a workers' movement emerged. Reflecting the transition between a tiny fraction of society and a large, growing force—an artisanal past versus a future of modern wage labor—the movement had no ready-made panaceas, no blueprints. Aided but also diverted by the activities of professional reformers, labor had ultimately to think its own way out of the prevailing ideological maze.

Activist workers regarded themselves as the foremost inheritors of the revolutionary republican tradition. Who more than they would have welcomed the printer Benjamin Franklin's advocacy of the four-hour work day, or shared his alarm at the "Disposition among some of our People to commence an Aristocracy, by giving to the Rich a predominance in Government"? When Thomas Jefferson insisted that "the earth belongs ... to the living, that the dead have neither powers nor rights over it," and that therefore no generation had the right to legislate for the next, many were prepared to take him at his word. Those whose fathers and grandfathers had fought and died in the War of Independence scorned the drift toward economic oligarchy as a violation of a cherished heritage, a repudiation of democracy's most precious values.

Certain utopian dreamers and organizers added to this legacy their own insights and inspiration. Robert Dale Owen and Frances Wright, publishers of the *Free Enquirer* newspaper, directors of a great open forum in New York City, and advocates of a sweeping transformation that they called "socialistic," for a time exerted considerable influence. Their emphasis on women's rights raised an issue little appreciated hitherto outside elite reform circles.

Notwithstanding these varied influences, the workers' own newspapers, books, pamphlets, and verses appearing in these years owe far more to experience than to any outside ideological source. One cannot help being struck by the freshness, humor, and free-spirited fearlessness with which the authors of this literature hurled themselves into the heart of things. With remarkable audacity and verve, these pioneers elaborated a thoroughgoing social critique, a program of action, and a vision of a desirable future. They recognized, as the *Mechanics' Free Press* noted in 1830, "two distinct classes: the rich and the poor, the oppressor and the oppressed, those that live by their own labor, and they that live by the labor of others." They were not content to ask for "a fair day's wage for a fair day's work." They saw farther and deeper, looking ahead to a Republic of Labor. If many of their notions could be described as utopian—and how could it have been otherwise, for those who ventured boldly onto unknown terrain?—theirs was very much a *workers'* utopia. Although they favored reforms, their ultimate goal was a "Radical Revolution" that would secure to each worker "the fruits of his toil." Before Karl Marx was even in his teens, the American labor movement as a whole was calling for the "abolition of wages-slavery." Workers dared to dream of a society without poverty, exploitation, drudgery, and war, a society founded on freedom and equality in which men, women, and children of all races could live in creative harmony, enjoying the good things of life.

WORKINGMEN'S POLITICS

These notions found their first important expression in the rise of Workingmen's parties. Starting in Philadelphia in 1828, the movement spread to every state. Workingmen's parties flourished in dozens of cities, and some fifty newspapers in at least fifteen states took up their program. Opposed to both major parties, which they saw as instruments of the oppressing class, Workingmen devised their own platforms and chose their own candidates. "Past experience," one such group declared, "teaches that we have nothing to hope from the aristocratic orders in society; and that our only course to pursue is, to send men of our own description, if we can, to the Legislature."

The wide-ranging immediate demands of Workingmen's parties included free public education; a direct system of election; reform of the civil service; simplification of the legal system; more equitable taxation; pensions for Revolutionary War veterans; and abolition of monopolies, lotteries, imprisonment for debt, capital punishment, child labor, and the prevailing militia system. Among their other goals were universal suffrage, a shorter workday, free trade, peace with the Indians, and the abolition of all slavery. They agitated, too, for better working conditions, more adequate sanitation facilities, and improved housing.

The new movement's most characteristic rallying cry, however, was for free land. One of American labor's earliest demands, it soon loomed larger than all others and retained its preeminence for decades. Land redistribution was already implicit in Langton Byllesby's *Observations on the Sources and Effects of Unequal Wealth* (1826). Three years later Thomas Skidmore vehemently called for land reform in *The Rights of Man to Property!* "Free public land to actual settlers" was a lifelong battle cry of George Henry Evans, the acknowledged "thinker of the Working Men's

Party" and editor of *The Working Man's Advocate,* the most widely read and influential labor paper of its day. All the way to the Civil War and even beyond, "Free land!" was a shibboleth of the militant labor movement. The struggle for land reform was as characteristic of the first epoch of organized labor in America as the struggle for the eight-hour day would be a half-century later, or the struggle for industrial unionism a half-century after that.

Because the question of land is so rarely raised in our own time, one may well wonder how it came to be the preoccupation of American labor for so many years. The fact is that in those days the public domain included by far the largest part of what is now the United States. The federal government's vast and increasing acquisition of territory to the west inevitably led people to ask, Who has the right to these millions of acres of sparsely occupied land—the working men and women who would live and labor there? Or monopolists and speculators who, without leaving their mansions back East, could become owners of immense regions merely by passing someone a few dollars?

For many leaders of the Workingmen's party, as for the much larger and more radical land reform movement that succeeded it, land was not something that could be legitimately bought or sold. Rather, it belonged to those who used it. "The right to the soil," they argued, "is as natural and equal as the right to light and air." They saw in the public domain a rare historic opportunity to avoid the extreme inequalities of social stratification that so disfigured civilization in Europe. By making America's western land available free to settlers, the surplus laboring population of the eastern cities would be steadily absorbed. Land reform thus would automatically eliminate wage cuts and unemployment, eventually raising wages and shortening the workday.

The new movement's universal and egalitarian character was especially evident in its relationship to other more impoverished and disfranchised sectors of the population. Workingmen's parties were led, for the most part, by native-born skilled craftsmen, English-speaking white males. But to a remarkable degree they extended their hands in cooperation and fellowship toward working women, the foreign born, slaves, native Americans, and the unskilled laborers of the new factories and mills. In short, they sought not merely to claim their share but also to take responsibility for civilization as a whole. For that very reason they constituted a serious threat to the political, financial, and industrial leadership of the emerging order.

The employers' political parties and the press branded the new movement with epithets then regarded as extreme: "infidels," "Jacobins," or the "Dirty Shirt" party. Each major party accused Workingmen of being agents of the other. For demanding free public education for children, Workingmen were accused of fomenting anarchy. For demanding the ten-hour day, they were accused of seeking to set up the guillotine. Again and again they were brought to court for "conspiring" to organize unions or to call strikes, both of which were against the law. Again and again they were set upon by the whole machinery of government, including the militia. The use of troops against labor, practically unknown in earlier years, now became more common.

The ability of reform (or pseudo-reform) politicians to confuse the issues and divert workingmen's votes ultimately proved even more damaging. From the start, in 1829—when the New York Workingmen's party polled some 6,000 votes and elected a carpenter to the state assembly—intrigues and manipulation provoked internal dissension and jeopardized the possibility of long-run accomplishment. As is still the case today, political parties, alarmed at the rapid growth of an opposition, grafted bits and pieces of Workingmen's programs onto their own platforms. In less populated districts, such as Newcastle County, Pennsylvania, wily politicians often succeeded in limiting Workingmen's access to the ballot.

On a deeper level, the ambiguity of the workingmen's own status in the nation rendered a sustained effort impossible. Class structure and regionalism reached a new level of flux. Well into the 1830s (albeit with greater difficulty each year), a journeyman printer could still set up his own shop or, if he preferred, take up farming, or acting, or sailing. Those who tired of the constant battle for a living wage could pull up stakes and try their luck out West. The new immigration of Irish labor and the ruin of some major manufactures—notably the hand-loom weaving of Philadelphia—added still more pressure to the already unstable constituent base.

The appeal of Andrew Jackson's Democratic party must be understood in this context. Workingmen's party leaders denounced many policies associated with Old Hickory's regime: its large-scale corruption and demagoguery, its promotion of genocidal war against native Americans, its commendation of slavery as part of the natural order of things. George Henry Evans, labor's most dedicated editor and penetrating theorist, attacked the infamous Indian Removal Act of 1830 which led to the tragic "Trail of Tears," the forced march of whole tribes from their ancestral lands in the Southeast to barren country over a thousand miles to the west. The states, he wrote, had "no more right to jurisdiction over the territory of the Cherokees than we have to be King of France." Tracing the origin of the Indian wars to land speculation, Evans argued that these wars would cease "if there were no encroachments on lands needed by the Indians for their subsistence." Emphasizing his solidarity with native Americans, Evans emblazoned as a motto on the front page of his paper a statement on land by the Sauk chief Black Hawk, and he reprinted material from a tribal paper, *The Cherokee Phoenix.*

Likewise, however much they may have disagreed (tactically and otherwise) with the abolitionists, Evans and other Workingmen's leaders continually pronounced slavery a hideous evil. At the time of Nat Turner's slave insurrection of 1831, when the nation's press resounded with outcries of fear and rage, and when even many abolitionists recoiled in horror, Evans penned a stirring defense of the revolt.

Despite all this criticism, Jacksonians represented themselves as foes of the monopolists, as advocates of cheap money for western farmers, and as champions of reform in the condition of labor. Proclaiming themselves the enemies of labor's enemies, local Jacksonian politicians steadily drained the life from Workingmen's electoral campaigns. Many of Workingmen's leaders actually endorsed Jackson, and most of them supported his battle against the tight-money U.S. Bank. In the political disintegration that followed the Workingmen's defeat, many party members lapsed into the regionalist and nativist tendencies of the 1840s signaled by Jackson's novel political realignment. Then, as since, the Democratic party picked up the pieces. But the true spirit of the Workingmen's movement stood outside these maneuvers.

The workday is no longer from sunrise to sundown; people are no longer jailed for debt; children, no longer forced to work in factories or mines, now learn to read and write in free public schools. For all these things we have ultimately to thank the Workingmen rather than major party politicians. Short-lived though Workingmen's parties were, they left indelible traces of their heroic passage. They imposed, for the first time, the *presence* of the working class as a crucial factor in American political life. If the parties themselves soon vanished, that presence has remained and grown.

In addition, the Workingmen's movement instilled immeasurable confidence in working people across the land. It demonstrated how much workers could accomplish, and how swiftly, when they acted independently, relying on their own initiative and power. Most important, Workingmen gave powerful momentum to the trade union movement. In the few years following their parties' defeat but preceding the Panic of 1837, workers joined unions by the tens of thousands. Nothing is more in the order of things than the fact that the leaders of this widespread unionization included many who had fought under the banner of the Workingmen's party.

Striking shoemakers parade in 1860, under the banner "American Ladies Will Not Be Slaves." Detail from *Leslie's Illustrated Weekly*. From Schnapper, *American Labor*.

Workers and Slavery

Eric Foner

America's first labor movement emerged in the same decade—the 1830s—in which slavery became a central focus of the nation's political life. Like other Americans, workingmen and women were forced to confront the contradiction between the professed ideals of the American nation and the existence of the South's "peculiar institution."

The continued existence of second-class status for blacks more than a century after the abolition of slavery changes the terms but not the essence of this contradiction between racism and equality, which lies in the slavery period.

As it developed in the 1830s and 1840s, the attitude of northern working people toward slavery was ambiguous. Like other Northerners, workers saw slavery as a violation of the principles of equality and liberty enunciated in the Declaration of Independence and central to American political culture. But relations between the fledgling labor movement and abolitionists were often difficult and strained.

Ironically, severe critics of labor relations in the North developed simultaneously in two very different movements—proslavery ideologues in the South, and labor leaders in the North. According to George Fitzhugh, John C. Calhoun, and other proslavery thinkers, the liberty of the northern wage earner was little more than the choice between selling his labor for a fraction of its true value or starving. In contrast to the southern slave, who was provided for in sickness and old age and never subjected to the tyranny of the marketplace, the free laborer of the North was a slave of the market, these writers insisted.

Northern workers, of course, were not likely to agree with Fitzhugh's conclusion that slavery was the best possible condition for all labor, white as well as black. But early labor leaders did agree that northern workers were not as much better off than the slaves as many believed. The phrase that entered the language of politics in the 1830s to describe the plight of the northern worker was "wage slavery." A comparison between the status of the northern worker and the southern slave—often to the detriment of the free worker—became a standard component of labor rhetoric in these years, and would remain so long after the abolition of slavery.

In language similar to that of the southern critics, the New England labor leader Seth Luther declared that northern factory workers toiled longer each day than did slave plantation workers. A New Hampshire labor newspaper asked, "A great cry is raised in the northern states against southern slavery. The sin of slavery may be abominable there, but is it not equally so here? If they have black slaves, have we not white ones?"

In New York City, when striking journeymen tailors were convicted of conspiracy in 1836, they issued the famous Coffin handbill, declaring, "The freemen of the North are now on a level with the slaves of the South."

"Wage slavery," of course, was not usually meant as a literal comparison of labor conditions North and South. But for those reared in the tradition of the independent artisan, working for wages seemed a form of slavery, for it entailed a loss of personal autonomy and of a sense of control over one's own destiny.

Workers who raised the cry of "wage slavery" were not indifferent to the evils of southern slavery. Many urban workers worried that emancipation of the slaves would unleash a flood of freedmen who might move north and challenge workers for jobs and status. Many workers shared the racism endemic throughout American society; their unions often excluded blacks from membership. But it was one thing to wish blacks to remain in the

South, and another to believe they should remain slaves. After all, the idea of wage slavery contained condemnation of slavery itself. The central values of the early labor movement—liberty, democracy, personal independence, the right of the worker to the fruits of his or her own labor—were obviously incompatible with the institution of slavery. And the intellectual fathers of the labor movement, Thomas Paine and Robert Dale Owen, were well known opponents of slavery.

It should not be surprising, therefore, that northern workers played a significant role in the movement against slavery. Thomas Wentworth Higginson, the Massachusetts abolitionist, later recalled that in Worcester the antislavery cause was "far stronger for a time in the factories and shoe shops than in the pulpits or colleges." In New York City the largest number of signers of abolitionist petitions in the 1830s were the city's artisans.

The radical artisans who met each year to celebrate Tom Paine's birthday usually included among their resolutions a denunciation of slavery and a salute to Haiti, where a black revolution had overthrown the slave system. By the same token, city merchants and early factory owners were likely to be hostile to the abolitionist cause, for their welfare was closely tied to trade with the South and the manufacture of textiles from slave-grown cotton.

Yet relations between the labor movement and abolitionism were not always friendly. In 1831 the very first issue of William Lloyd Garrison's *Liberator,* a militant voice of the antislavery cause, included an attack on northern labor reformers. "We are the friends of reform," Garrison wrote, "but this is not reform, which in curing one evil, threatens to inflict a thousand others." In response, the northern labor spokesman William West insisted that labor and abolition should work together. Each, he declared, was trying to secure from a group of laborers "the fruits of their toil."

During the 1840s the socialist reformer Albert Brisbane called on abolitionists to attack the exploitation of wage workers in the North. But most abolitionists, themselves property owners, accepted northern labor relations as natural and just. The labor movement, expressing an ideal with roots in the republican tradition of the American Revolution, equated freedom with ownership of productive property. The wage earner, in their view, was not truly free because his livelihood was dependent on the will of others. The abolitionist movement, by contrast, developed a new notion of freedom, equating it simply with self-ownership, that is, not being a slave.

LABOR AND ANTISLAVERY

During the 1840s a handful of abolitionist spokesmen, moving toward a critique of the plight of northern labor, attempted to forge an alliance with labor leaders. Nathaniel Rogers, the editor of a New Hampshire newspaper, proposed a grand alliance of the "producing classes"—southern slaves and northern workers—against exploiters of labor in both sections. Living amidst the expanding factory system of New England, Rogers concluded, "We have got to look to the working people of the North, to sustain and carry on the Anti-Slavery movement."

At the same time, several labor leaders and political figures sympathetic to labor—such as George Henry Evans, the English labor reformer now living in the United States, and Horace Greeley, the editor of the New York *Tribune*—sought to link the interests of labor and antislavery in a different way. The labor movement had been devastated by the depression of 1837–42, and when it reemerged in the 1840s its focus was on land reform. Evans, Greeley, and many others concluded that "land monopoly" was the root of the problems of northern labor. The solution was the Homestead plan—every person who so desired should receive 160 acres of free public land from the federal government. This would enable eastern workers to escape "wage slavery" altogether, by establishing their economic independence on farms in the West. Those who remained behind would benefit from the reduction in the number of laborers, which would lead to wage increases. Land reform would thus solve the problem of urban poverty and offer every workingman the opportunity to achieve independence.

The homestead idea ("free soil," as it came to be called) was implicitly antislavery because free homesteads could not coexist with large plantations manned by slaves. For such a proposal to be put into effect, the spread of slavery into the western territories had to be barred.

In 1848 a coalition of antislavery politicians and labor leaders formed the Free Soil party, the first substantial third party committed to stopping the extension of slavery and to providing free land to settlers. The Free Soilers, with Van Buren as their candidate for president, polled 10 percent of the popular vote and won considerable support from labor organizations. The party placed slavery and free soil at the center stage of politics and began eliminating the breach between abolitionists and labor.

Previously, many abolitionists had seen labor's demands as diverting attention from the pressing needs of the southern slave, while labor leaders had often viewed abolition as a way of diverting interest from conditions in the North. Free Soil provided a platform on which antislavery men and the labor movement could join hands.

Slavery became the dominant issue in the North in the 1850s through Free Soilism, which provided common ground for the abolitionists' stress on the freedom of the individual and the labor movement's insistence that both southern slavery and northern wage slavery be attacked.

In the hands of the Republican party, which emerged as the dominant political force in the 1850s, the Free Soil version of antislavery laid its greatest stress on the differences between northern and southern conditions of labor. In Republican ideology, the hallmark of northern society was the laborer's opportunity for social mobility. In the South, not only the slave but also non-slaveholding whites were denied the opportunity to better their conditions. Wealth produced by the slave system flowed to a small aristocracy of slaveholders, while the great mass of southern blacks and whites remained impoverished. In the North, by

contrast, the opportunity to rise from the condition of wage
earner to that of independent artisan, farmer, or entrepreneur not
only defused class conflict but also spurred labor efficiency,
which produced the impressive economic progress enjoyed by
northern society.

No individual expressed what might be called the labor basis of
antislavery more effectively than Abraham Lincoln. His own life
exemplified the opportunities for social mobility offered by
northern society. From two fundamental premises of the labor
movement—the dignity of labor and the right of the laborer to
the full fruits of his or her own work—Lincoln fashioned a devas-
tating critique of slavery. Slavery, he said was simply robbery—
one person labored and another enjoyed the fruits. "I want every
man to have the chance—and I believe a black man is entitled to
it—in which he can better his condition," Lincoln declared.
Speaking of a black woman, he added, "In some respects she is
certainly not my equal, but in her natural right to eat the bread
she earns with her own hands without asking the leave of anyone
else, she is my equal and the equal of all others."

Lincoln thus demanded for blacks freedom to compete in
the marketplace, the right to take part in what he called "the
race of life." He assumed that anyone, black or white, who
worked diligently could achieve the cherished goal of economic independence.

Did northern labor support the Republican party in the 1850s?
Put this way, the question is impossible to answer, for northern
labor, like other groups in northern society, was divided along
lines of ethnicity, region, and occupation. The most exploited
segment of the working class—Irish immigrants in the urban
centers of the East and the factory towns of New England—was
solidly Democratic, for the Democratic party provided essential
services: jobs, housing, assistance with the law. On the other
hand, skilled urban workers, especially the native born, rallied to
the Republican banner. Artisans found in the Republican ideology an affirmation of their own position in northern society.
The center of Republican support was in rural areas of the North.

Yet here, too, along with farmers, were the small shops of many northern craftsmen who joined their agricultural neighbors to support Republicans. These men helped elect Lincoln to the presidency in 1860 and supported his resistance to compromise with the South in the secession crisis of 1860–61. On the issue of the expansion of slavery, northern laborers were inflexible, for to allow slavery to dominate the West would cut off what many saw as the main avenue of social advancement for themselves and their children.

WORKERS RALLY TO THE UNION

Thus the political movement against slavery enjoyed the support of many northern workers while articulating their aspirations. When the South fired upon Fort Sumter, northern labor rallied to support the Union, along with virtually all other elements of northern society. But the Civil War represented both a triumph and a tragedy for northern labor. The goal of abolition was finally achieved—not through moral persuasion, as favored by the abolitionists, but because of the exigencies of war and the efforts of the slaves themselves to escape their bondage.

The ranks of the Union army were filled by the farmers and laborers of the North. At the same time, however, northern labor increasingly came to resent the manner in which the war effort was being organized. Manufacturers and bond dealers made fortunes in government contracts while inflation eroded the incomes of workers, and the government on occasion intervened with troops to break strikes that it felt were injuring the war effort. Northern workers resented the draft law of 1863 that enabled men of wealth to buy their way out of the army. The result was a series of antidraft riots, most notably the New York draft riots of July 1863, which turned from a protest against the draft into a savage attack on the city's black residents.

The Civil War gave a tremendous boost to industrial expansion in the North and laid the foundation for the social conflicts of the Gilded Age. If the first large group of American millionaires came out of the Civil War, so too did a revitalized labor movement, proud of its part in the overthrow of slavery yet insisting that workers share in the fruits of the new industrial society. The idea of "wage slavery," which had been eclipsed in the 1850s, rose like a phoenix from the ashes of the Civil War to inspire the great crusades of the National Labor Union, the Knights of Labor, and other labor organizations in the post-war years.

Members of the Women's Trade Union League demonstrating in the Murray Hill section of Manhattan. From Schnapper, *American Labor*.

Women's Labor and Politics

Mari Jo Buhle

Composed mostly of college-educated women, today's women's movement represents an articulate and skilled sector of the workforce of advanced capitalism. The movement seeks to promote activity across sectoral and race lines, in battered women's shelters, in organizing drives among the "pink collar" office workers by such groups as Nine to Five, or in giving aid to labor organizations such as the Coalition of Labor Union Women. A commitment to equal treatment for women of all ranks has been the most coherent and sustained "politics" of women's activity.

The pioneer women activists of a century ago, if they could see today's efforts, would no doubt flash a smile of recognition. In their day women had been drawn to the workforce by another transition, from preindustrial to industrial labor. Like our contemporary activists, nineteenth-century militants believed their middle-class status provided the strength of education, relative leisure, and the responsibility for aiding and learning from women of the working class.

The first women activists faced many dilemmas. Denied the right to vote until 1920, women could not participate directly in politics. Neither could they establish themselves among the craft organizations of better-paid skilled workers. Yet, for many urban women, wage labor constituted at least one phase of their lives, and working women often sought alliances outside the unions.

From the launching of labor reform organizations in the 1830s to the proliferation of ameliorative institutions in the 1870s to the

31

agitation for women's unions and protective legislation in the 1880s and 1890s and the spectacular "women's strikes" of 1909–16, women workers reached across class lines to find the support they could obtain in no other way. Although these alliances were fraught with internal tension, women from various classes could agree on a common principle: equal treatment, equal pay for equal work.

FIRST STEPS AS WAGE EARNERS

American women began to rally behind this banner in the second quarter of the nineteenth century, when thousands of women first became wage earners in textile factories and the needle trades. As early as the 1830s many middle-class women aided their unemployed or destitute sisters who had been struck down by the vagaries of an early urban-industrial economy. Philanthropic activists formed societies to assist self-supporting wives with small children, elderly single women, and the mates of indigent husbands. They sponsored exchanges for women's work that allowed women with little industrial training to use traditional skills and find a market for handmade articles. They founded employment bureaus to locate reputable establishments and temporary lodging houses to assist women new to the city and in need of work.

During the financial crises of 1837 and 1857, many middle-class women who began as benefactors became recipients of aid. In Boston alone, some 2,500 needlewomen—grown to ten times that number in another decade—competed desperately for a living, often maintained only by the efforts of their sisters. Even in prosperous times, declining family fortunes or the death or desertion of a husband could deprive the most respectable housewife of her subsistence. Treading a narrow line between charity and self-help, these benevolent institutions spoke in a common voice for every woman's right to rise above her precarious situation, to participate fully in civil society and to labor with dignity for her own bread.

The textile mill operatives in Lowell, Massachusetts, in the 1830s–40s came from a different direction but espoused similar principles. "If any are in want," they knew, "the Ladies will be compassionate and assist them." Working women, however, preferred to be their own agents. In the "mother of industries," America's first major factory experiment, women comprised nearly 60 percent of the 67,000 textile workers in 1830. They reacted to declining wages with their own protests, and in 1844 they organized the Lowell Female Reform Association and became a major force in the ten-hour movement that spread across New England. Attached to the labor movement, these women also addressed their particular plight as female workers. Like the middle-class activists, they spoke often in the name of sisterhood.

Initiated at the behest of both working women and middle-class activists, a vigorous discussion of women's position in the labor market commenced shortly before the Civil War. The rise of a distinct crusade for women's rights—for suffrage, marriage reform, and property rights—beginning with the famous meeting at Seneca Falls, New York, in 1848 and spreading throughout the 1850s added fuel to this fire.

By 1860, a noteworthy feminist treatise laid out the basic principles. "Women want to work for all the reasons men want it," affirmed Caroline Dall in the landmark publication *Women's Right to Labor.* Men professed to encourage domestic happiness but actually promoted a destructive idleness among the middle class while driving poor women to despair. It was as if, Dall complained, men had dictated to women, "Marry, stitch, die or do worse." Women had to organize to confront this injustice. Sister to sister, they had to battle for respect and dignity; for their right to labor and to develop their full range of talents; to escape penury and prostitution; to do away once and for all with the pernicious myth that "all men support all women" in favor of economic equality.

Social dislocations fostered by the Civil War gave this discussion a pressing urgency. During the recession of the late 1850s, the poverty of working women was widespread. The introduction of the sewing machine also had a detrimental effect: driven by family poverty to pick up their needles, women found piece rates lowered and fluctuating wildly. The draft of many thousands of male breadwinners during the Civil War deepened the crisis. Even the boom and an upsurge of trade unionism at the end of the war left women on the margins.

For a brief historical moment, mainstream labor seemed to reach out toward the women's cause. The National Labor Union, founded in 1866, placed itself on record for the "individual and undivided support to the sewing women, factory operatives, and daughters of toil" required for the solidarity of labor against capital's wage-cutting offensives. At a moment when women held some 20 percent of the rapidly growing number of industrial jobs (closer to 30 percent in the most industrialized sector of the nation, New England), this was elementary self-defense. Only one affiliated union, the Cigar Makers, admitted individual women to membership, but the NLU gesture encouraged some reformers— led by the suffrage pioneer Susan B. Anthony—to proclaim an alliance of women and labor in a popular feminist weekly, *The Revolution,* and to form branches of a Working Women's Association in New York.

The reformers' efforts proved fruitless, however. In the end, the NLU expelled Anthony under pressure from the printers' union and devastated the alliance. For their part, women activists retreated to philanthropy and sisterly self-help. Disappointed in their would-be male collaborators, feminists drew the painful conclusion that working women required their own institutions collectively administered by members of their own sex.

Over the next quarter-century the women's movement spread across the country as it organized to assist women in their struggles for a livelihood or for a professional career. In the late 1880s delegates at a major meeting of women's groups officially adopted their cardinal principle: "Equal wages for equal work."

Institutions that had begun before the Civil War proliferated. All major cities boasted a network of protective societies providing legal services to women cheated in wage contracts; boarding homes such as those operated by the Young Women's Christian Association; free or inexpensive classes to teach skills including clerical, domestic, carpentry, and design; employment bureaus; emergency assistance programs for unemployed women or victims of domestic violence; social clubs.

One important contribution of the women's movement was the pioneering investigation of the conditions of women's labor conducted by Virginia Penny, Susan B. Anthony, and newly organized women's clubs. The New England Women's Club investigation of Boston's needlewomen became a model for the first exhaustive study by the Massachusetts bureau of the statistics of labor, published in 1884. Women's groups in other cities, fostered the study of sweatshop labor and exposed unhealthy conditions in the garment, cigar and cigarette, and other light manufactures that employed mostly women and children.

In aiding women wage earners, middle-class activists did not generally strive to foster working-class solidarity, nor did they promote trade unionism. Rather, they blessed individual achievement and held out the American dream of upward mobility. But they did believe that sex discrimination in the marketplace could best be confronted by organized women.

Such was the case in Chicago, where the local women's movement regularly fed activists into trade union struggles. A short-lived working women's society in the 1870s joined such labor notables as Lucy Parsons with middle- and working-class women. Middle-class organizations like the Women's Christian Temperance Union established formal ties with the Knights of Labor, while the WCTU's socialist president Frances Willard promised Grand Master Workman Terence Powderly her full cooperation.

In the late 1880s a grand coalition took shape. The Illinois Woman's Alliance was the organizational child of Elizabeth Morgan, purportedly the first woman to join the Chicago Knights of Labor and founder of the Ladies' Federal Labor Union, and Corrine Brown, a prominent educator with roots deep in the women's movement. Bringing together activists from

trade unions, the Socialist Labor party, and the women's movement, the IWA not only promoted trade unionism among women
but also waged a massive political campaign on their behalf.
Under Morgan's direction, the IWA conducted a massive sur-
vey of sweatshops and formulated model laws for compulsory
education and the regulation of conditions in establishments
employing women and children. The IWA also secured positions
for women as factory inspectors who would faithfully enforce
these laws. Other campaigns pressured the school board to add
more women members and to erect more schools in poor neighborhoods, secured public bathhouses in working-class neighborhoods and defended the legal rights of streetwalking prostitutes.
    But the IWA, like many other institutions supported by the
women's movement, could not survive the class and ethnic
conflicts of the 1890s. Like most labor and populist movements,
it succumbed to defeat. Native-born activists steeped in republican values—individualism, temperance, and class reconciliation—
could scarcely comprehend, let alone work easily with, "new
immigrants" from Eastern and Southern Europe. The severe
depression of the 1890s also widened the distance between the
classes and provoked fears of bloody conflict. The times could
not sustain the simple faith in sisterhood.
    Yet this legacy persisted. The first decade of the twentieth cen-
tury brought a further dramatic increase in women's wage labor.
Women entered former male preserves such as commerce, transportation, and communication and predominated in such trades
as steam laundries, retail sales, food processing, and many
branches of light manufacturing, above all in garments. Labor
participation was especially high among first- and second-
generation immigrants: nearly 60 percent of these women aged
18–24 worked for wages in New York City in 1910. These
upsurges fostered new hopes for women's advancement and
moved women activists once more toward a cross-class alliance:
the Women's Trade Union League.
    Drawing upon important veterans of the 1880s and early
1890s, the WTUL organized in 1903 as a curiously hybrid institu-

tion halfway between the American Federation of Labor and the women's movement. Its intention was to hitch the potential of women workers to the public influence and institutional power of middle-class "allies." The WTUL sponsored factory legislative bills, encouraged greater self-awareness among working women, and promoted union organization.

The New York shirtwaist makers' strikes, "The Uprising of 20,000," marked a turning point in the history of the WTUL. From November 1909 through February 1910, young women workers tied up the garment industry, only to find the International Ladies' Garment Workers Union too feeble to respond adequately. Until that time the ILGWU had few women members and even slimmer financial resources and was simply ill equipped to manage a general strike. The WTUL and local socialist women thus played decisive roles from the first days as they threw themselves into strike support. These sympathizers sat behind the tables and enrolled women into the union, raised funds and provided publicity, walked the picket lines and went to jail with the strikers. The WTUL grew strong in this situation. Although the shirtwaist makers did not win their major demand for a union shop, they had planted the seeds for permanent unionism in the garment trade, for women and men alike.

Over the next decade, working women joined by various allies staged impressive union drives. In 1910 Chicago garment workers supported by women in the WTUL, the Socialist party, and the settlement movement brought production in the menswear industry to a standstill and laid the basis for the Amalgamated Clothing Workers. In 1912, at Lawrence, Massachusetts, socialist women shouldered the burden of strike support; Margaret Sanger and other New York women organized the removal of the strikers' children, while the Wobbly hero Elizabeth Gurley Flynn earned her title "Rebel Girl." By 1920 women working in white goods, in department stores, in telephone operations, and elsewhere established the first unions in their trades.

At their peak, working women's organizations in the second decade of the twentieth century embraced a panoply of programs designed to meet various aspects of women's situation. Socialist women cooperating with both the suffrage and the labor movements helped push through the woman suffrage referendums in the Western states; in alliance with the WTUL, socialists conducted the all-out suffrage drive in New York during 1915 and 1917. The broadest spectrum of women's groups, from suffrage to settlement house, labor and socialist, formed a united front to protest against American entry into World War I. Once the war came home, union women with their neighborhood supporters formed consumers' groups to battle inflation's ravages and to place the onus of price increases upon the profiteers. Finally, but by no means least important, working-class women behind socialist leadership rallied for the right to disseminate birth-control information.

Cut short by vicious government censorship and the jailing of militants, such activities nevertheless succeeded in summing up the experiences of nearly a century. The mainstream labor movement neither could nor would supply the necessary context for addressing a broad range of issues peculiar to working women's situation. For better or worse, a coalition of women contributed the framework of political reform and ameliorative institutions imbued with sex-conscious idealism. At its most dynamic, the effort also helped make possible a successful women's unionism.

The distinctive tradition of women's labor organization carried within itself deep contradictions from its inception. Tensions over class perspectives and goals rose again and again. The difficulties became most painfully apparent during the heroic strike campaigns. At the high point of the 1909 shirtwaist makers' strike, for example, political disagreements threatened to destroy the uneasy alliance of women. If class-conscious radicals insisted on explaining to the public that all woes stemmed from capitalist oppression, the financial "angels" who paid many of the WTUL's bills sought to make suffrage rather than socialism, the emancipation of a sex rather than a class, the lesson of the day.

The WTUL never did succeed in eradicating an aura of condescension on the part of its "allies," nor did it sort out the significance of various aspects of its program—unionism, legislative reform, and social services—in relation to the class struggle. In one sense, it replicated the dilemma inherent from the beginning. Middle-class women, however sympathetic to the working woman's cause, always tended to prefer ameliorative programs such as protective legislation over unionism. Working women and socialists, disdaining patronage and fearful of isolation from the labor movement, lacked the resources to devise a viable alternative.

The legacy of the sisterly alliance remains a significant historical phenomenon. Although women gained full political rights in 1920 and eventually won greater recognition from the mainstream labor movement, they remain at the bottom of the labor force. So, too, the reality of sex discrimination has continued to cut, however unequally, across class and race lines and to raise persistent questions about working women's ultimate destiny. Equal treatment, equal pay for equal work—so simple an idea, so elementary in a democratic context—remains an unrealized goal.

A poster for the United Labor party, one of many local workingmen's parties in the 1870s-'80s. From Schnapper, *American Labor*.

Paths to Power after the Civil War

Alan Dawley

No single political aim, philosophy, or party animates the American working class. Labor's political strategies vary widely, from nonpartisanship to a labor party to close alliance with the Democrats. If there is a common thread running through these diverse practices, it is the very inheritance of struggle itself. Excluded from power—even in the democratic system that professes to allow no such exclusion by class or condition—working people have been compelled to battle for the right to organize, to speak freely, and to advance their interests against hostile employers and entrenched authorities. Success has not come easy or often.

The period after the Civil War is a case in point. Giant monopolies were springing up in railroads, oil, and steel. Mine owners and railroad magnates were dead set against unions, driving potential unionists into secret organizations such as the Mollie Maguires. An arrogant lot of Robber Barons showered contempt on the public and their employees alike. "The public be damned," said Commodore Vanderbilt. "I can hire half the working class to shoot the other half," said Jay Gould. This upstart oligarchy of predatory wealth came to dominate national politics. It hunkered down behind the gold standard, high tariffs, laissez-faire, and the militia, and it shut out the working population, which was growing increasingly numerous and restive. Forced to break new paths to power, the labor movement, for its part, pushed forward in several directions at once. One path led to an independent Labor party; another led away from electoral politics altogether toward anarchism and direct action. By far the largest group moved toward nonpartisan social reform, a combination of education, community organization, and labor lobbying best represented by the Knights of Labor, which was 750,000 strong at its peak.

The origins of nonpartisan reform lie in the disintegration of the grand coalition that had supported the Union cause in the Civil War. Northern workers had been a vital part of the coalition, and so long as there remained a threat of renewed planter aggression they supported Republican policies. Thus when southern planters enacted "black codes" that restored everything about slavery but the name, most working people backed the Radical Republicans in Congress, who took command of the federal government from pro-planter President Andrew Johnson and sent Union troops back into the South to protect freed slaves.

Still, sympathy for the plight of blacks was tempered by suspicion of the businessmen who acted as their benefactors. Labor leaders sometimes complained that the slaves had been freed while northern wage earners remained "wage slaves."

One sign of worker disaffection with business leadership in politics was the National Labor Union. Founded in 1866 with an iron molder named William Sylvis as its leading light, the NLU signaled a new stage in working-class organization. It was the first nationwide expression of a community of interest among wage earners, though it also maintained friendly relations with farmers and other producers. It campaigned for government Greenbacks, expulsion of speculators from public land, and the eight-hour day, which it won for federal employees.

The NLU was part of a larger movement of labor reform that combatted evil by exhorting or legislating against it. Labor reformers such as Terence Powderly, Grand Master Workman of the Knights of Labor, combined a sacred reverence for the ballot with a philosophy of laissez-faire. Reformers believed that the chief task for a political officeholder was to avoid corruption—no mean feat when railroad tycoons bragged about bribing legislators on the installment plan, $1,000 down and $1,000 more when their bill passed. Every big city had its city hall gang, of which the

Tweed Ring in New York was the most infamous. They saw to it that big contributors could go about their business unmolested. In return for labor votes, urban bosses paid off in jobs and favors, first to keep city unions weak, later to keep them quiet. Thus the field was controlled by well-entrenched Republican or Democratic machines by the time labor reformers entered the battle. Their high-minded rhetoric (they were forever appealing to temperance and manliness) and their nonpartisan stance (vote for the man, not the party) were not just moral postures but also calculated efforts to detach labor voters from the saloonkeeper and ward leader (often the same man) who ran the party's machine.

Reformers looked forward to the eventual abolition of "wage slavery." Believing that labor was the source of all wealth, they envisoned a time when labor would own the wealth it produced and industry would be run cooperatively. Ira Steward, a self-educated Boston machinist, worked out the details of the transition to cooperation through the eight-hour day. He reasoned that shortening hours would reduce the time the laborer worked to enrich his employer, and, once the eight-hour day became universal, the laborer would be working exclusively for himself. In short, labor and capital would merge. This hoped-for harmony accounts for the enormous popularity of Edward Bellamy's utopian novel *Looking Backward,* a fantasy of cooperative production and distribution in the ideal city of the future.

The gap between noble aspiration and practical achievement was, inevitably, large. A Labor Reform party entered the field, elected a handful of candidates, mostly in Massachusetts, and then disappeared. The eight-hour movement gained several state laws in addition to the federal statute, but legalizing the eight-hour day meant nothing without enforcement.

This emergence of labor as a self-conscious political entity fostered a realignment of political forces that culminated with the end of Reconstruction in 1877. Politics had turned for more than a generation around a North-South axis. A new axis pitted farmers and workers against big business. The Republican coalition began to disintegrate in the face of labor reformers' demands, and it crumbled further when immigrant workers, notably the Irish, moved into the Democratic party and midwestern farmers pushed through state laws governing railroad freight rates. Radical Republicans, fast reaching the end of their Reconstruction agenda, were unwilling to add southern agrarian reform to their list. Unalterably opposed to property in slaves, they were passionately devoted to property in just about everything else. Confiscating planter estates for wholesale redistribution to former slaves was not a priority.

When the Democrats won the popular vote in 1876 and held the presidency hostage for a Republican promise to pull federal troops out of the South, the Republicans relinquished their hold on the South in return for the presidency. In effect, northern businessmen and southern planters put aside their differences in order to make a common defense of property interests.

It was none too soon. Six months after the Compromise of 1877, the country was convulsed by the biggest strike ever, touched off by railroad wage cuts. Tens of thousands of people struck; dozens were killed, and millions of dollars in property was destroyed. The new Republican president, Rutherford B. Hayes, sent in federal troops recently withdrawn from the South to put down the strike. The ensuing realignment of political forces kept the working class isolated from national influence for the next quarter-century. That, in turn, compelled working people to embark on a search for new solutions to labor's wrongs. The most important of the new organizations was the Knights of Labor. Not only did the Knights enroll more members than anyone else, but they also confronted head on the huge combines that were monopolizing the nation's railroads, mines, and mills. They led strikes against Jay Gould's railroad system and conducted a massive educational campaign against the predatory values of acquisitive individualism, counterposing the brotherhood of the Knights—men and women, skilled and unskilled, black and white—to the greedy ambitions of the Robber Barons. Their encounter with the power of monopoly forced them to drop their laissez-faire assumptions and to adopt demands for public regulations; in the case of railroads, they also demanded public ownership of the means of production. Firmly wedded to the nonpartisan philosophy, they neither courted Democrats or Republicans nor created an independent labor party. Instead, they waged a massive education campaign in dozens of labor journals such as the *Labor Enquirer* and the *Knights of Labor,* organized community boycotts against "foul" employers, and lobbied public officials on behalf of cheap money and short hours. Although they did not survive in the twentieth century, failure is not their epitaph. They taught a generation of Americans that the nobility of toil is not merely a pious phrase, that the whole of industrial civilization rests on the producers.

Most radical of the emerging groups were the Social Revolutionaries, who combined anarchist hatred for the state with syndicalist faith in workers' ability to take power on their own. Founded by a splinter of the Socialist Labor party, they joined forces with Johann Most and the International Working People's Association in 1881. Bloody suppression of the 1877 strikes engendered popular hatred for government authorities, especially for the Coal and Iron Police and the Pinkerton guards, who often did the dirty work. Social Revolutionaries gave vent to these feelings and expressed the bitterness toward economic exploitation felt by many German and Bohemian immigrants, who were the largest contingents in their ranks. In German-speaking neighborhoods of Cincinnati and St. Louis, wood-carvers, typographers, and other working people with a little classical education, a love for romantic literature and a touch of atheism, organized sports competitions, music festivals and galas for the IWPA. Newspapers such as the Chicago *Arbeiter Zeitung* (Workers Journal) were the nerve centers of the movement, through which, in secret code, the armed units of the Lehr und Wehr Vereine (Educational and Fighting Union) were mustered. In Chicago a large German membership in the Central Labor Union gave Social Revolutionaries a critical leadership role. In the heavily native and Irish Knights of Labor, however, they were hounded out for being anarchists.

Anarchism is commonly confused with many things it is not. It is not chaos, rugged individualism, or violence. These were the features of the existing order that anarchists condemned. Rather, anarchists stood for unremitting opposition to constituted authority and aimed at a society without police, judges, prisons, armies or kings; in short, without a state. The Social Revolutionaries' goal of a self-governing community of equal producers had something in common with the labor reformers' cooperative commonwealth, but there the resemblance ended.

Anarchists put down the reformers' faith in the ballot as a miserable delusion. This rejection of the ballot as "the sum total of all humbugs" was one reason why the appeal of the Social Revolutionaries was limited. Another was their call for armed self-defense and the distortions of their views on violence. American anarchists actually committed few violent deeds, but they did study the *Science of Revolutionary Warfare* and exhorted the unemployed to learn the use of explosives, with little more result than to encourage the stereotype of the anarchist as a bearded, half-crazed conspirator skulking about with dynamite bombs stuffed in his coat pockets.

The anarchist doctrine of "propaganda by the deed," originated by the Russian nobleman Peter Kropotkin, was enacted in Europe with bombs, knives, and revolvers on a string of princes and monarchs from Spain to Russia. It reached the United States with a botched attempt on the life of Henry Clay Frick and the assassination of President William McKinley in 1901. In the poorer regions of Europe, the intellectual's doctrine of violence against the state combined with the peasant's violence against landlords to give anarchism a popular base in the emerging labor movement. In the United States, however, despite vigilantism, lynch laws, and high homicide rates, the doctrine ran up against a widespread feeling that the republic belonged to the people. Violence against the nation's symbols and leaders tended to deprive anarchists of support.

The revolutionary movement of this period climaxed in the May 1886 strike for the eight-hour day. Nothing like it had ever been seen before. Upwards of a quarter-million workers took part, beginning May 1, in actions that combined the spontaneity of insurrectionary crowds with the discipline of industrial organization. Reaching the proportions of a nationwide general strike, it was the most significant American contribution to the international working class. This event is commemorated in May Day. As first-rate agitators, the Social Revolutionaries came into their own in this heady atmosphere of mass protest. Their influence multiplied far beyond their numbers, and they found themselves—like the Industrial Workers of the World, in textile strikes twenty-five years later, and the Communist party in the Congress of Industrial Organizations of the 1930s—leading masses of people who were not necessarily in sympathy with their revolutionary arms.

On the fourth day of the 1886 strike a bomb was thrown into a detachment of police who were dispersing a peaceable crowd listening to speeches in Chicago's Haymarket Square. Business and civic leaders immediately charged that the dead policemen were victims of "propaganda of the deed" and called for anarchist blood. Later, the trial of eight anarchists became a travesty of justice. Although they were convicted of murder, no evidence was introduced to show that the defendants had either thrown a bomb (some were not even at the scene) or told someone else to do it. The actual perpetrator was never produced in court. Nevertheless, four were hanged, including the two most prominent Social Revolutionaries in Chicago, August Spies and Albert Parsons. With the state behaving the way anarchist theory said it would, their movement might have been expected to gain strength. Instead, it disappeared within a year. Having ridden the crest of the eight-hour strike, it went down with it.

INDEPENDENT POLITICAL ACTION

Independent political action addressed the same post–1877 conditions but through the electoral process. Built on the Knights of Labor's proselytizing of the antimonopoly philosophy, independent political action sought to put a distinct working-class program on the political agenda. The two major parties had turned their backs on labor goals, including an eight-hour law with teeth, abolition of the truck system, government ownership

of transportation and communication, and municipal ownership of street railways and public works. This strategy conceded
the virtue of the electoral process while going beyond the mere
election of incorruptible candidates to insist on the enactment of
pro-labor laws and policies. It was represented by a string of new
parties—socialist, farmer-labor, workingmen—culminating in
the United Labor party of 1886.

Outside the ranks of socialists and anarchists, for whom the
enemy was capitalism, the labor movement defined the enemy as
monopoly—bank capital, corporate finance, and big business of
any sort. Labor's most radical demand was government ownership of the railroads, which, as the leading capitalist institutions
of the day, stood atop a pyramid of investment in mining, communication, manufacturing, and real estate. The role of the
banks was to be curtailed by substituting greenbacks for private
currency. Great wealth was to be repossessed by an income tax.
Land speculators and absentee owners would have their property
confiscated, with land titles going only to actual settlers.

Antimonopoly was behind several third-party campaigns. The
Greenback-Labor party inaugurated the fight for a peoples'
money in 1878. Gathering a million votes two years later, the
party reorganized for a less successful effort in 1884 under the
People's party label.

The most significant of these third parties was the United
Labor party of 1886. It was a remarkable coalition of all the main
currents of the labor movement—labor reformers from the
Knights of Labor, trade unionists such as Samuel Gompers of the
newly formed American Federation of Labor, socialists, diehard
Greenbackers, eight-hour men, and the Single Tax followers of
Henry George, who headed the ticket in New York. This unac-
customed unity was imposed on the movement by the special
conditions of the moment—the strike wave, the major parties'
subservience to plutocracy, the judicial lynching of the Haymarket anarchists, the assassination of strikers by Gould's mer-
cenary army—all of which momentarily fused the inchoate class
consciousness of American workers into a unified movement.

The ULP did not do badly for a first try—George came in

second, ahead of Theodore Roosevelt. But after the election the various factions quickly fell to squabbling. George declared unequivocally against socialism, Gompers repudiated independent political action and turned nonpartisan, and the Socialist Labor party regretted its temporary antimonopoly indiscretion. Independent political action was dead for the time being, but it had gone further toward giving the democratic process a working-class content than any of its predecessors, and it left its legacy for the future. The "gas and water socialism" of the 1890s enacted ULP platforms. The Sherman Antitrust Act was a victory for the antimonopoly principle, though a pyrrhic one—its first use was against the American Railway Union, not a railroad trust. The Populist party took up the fight against monopoly and passed it to the next generation.

CONCLUSION

The nineteenth-century labor movement reached its peak in the mid-1880s. By no coincidence, that was when it pressed its claims against capital through independent political action. By comparison, the nonpartisan strategy of Powderly was the timidity of immaturity, while the nonpartisan stance of Gompers was the timidity of weakness.

Working-class politics in these years responded to exclusion from power. As President Cleveland's use of troops to break the railroad strike of 1894 showed, labor had no influence in Washington. Not until the New Deal would workers join another grand coalition as they had joined the Republican party during the Civil War, in a move that would give them access to the highest circles of power.

In the meantime, the movement tried other strategies. "Reward your friends and punish your enemies" became the hallmark of the AFL. Independent working-class politics was taken up by the Socialist party. Antimonopoly was adopted by several farmer-labor groups. However the enemy was defined, the labor movement continued the search for the best means of defeating it.

One of many "stickerettes" for the Industrial Workers of the World, which were pasted on telephone poles, store windows, etc. From Schnapper, *American Labor*.

Socialists and Wobblies

Paul Buhle

How can a committed Socialist minority in American politics escape the irrelevance of isolation, the confusion and corruption rampant in the two-party mainstream? Through the prism of one decisive historical experience—the first large-scale Socialist political movement in the U.S.—we may look for elements of an answer.

The Socialist party in its heyday made electoral socialism an option for substantial segments of the labor movement, on a scale not attained before or since. The party's influence cut across geographic and ethnic boundaries, sustained itself through repeated crises, and for a historic moment posed a threat to the two-party monopoly of power. The Socialists' strength may be ascribed to their faith in democracy. They believed in the vote as a symbol of the larger process of debate that would lead to enlightened public involvement. Their weakness lay in the ability of their enemies—corporations, mainstream politicians, and anti-Socialist reformers—to use that process to their own ends and in the difficulty of labor and its allies to exercise the immense potential at hand.

ORIGINS

The roots of the Socialist movement lie in the turmoil of the 1880s and 1890s, which sharpened the social conflicts in the United States while eliminating other radical alternatives. After

1886 the Knights of Labor and the German-dominated anarchist and socialist movements receded, leaving the field to the American Federation of Labor and the scattering of reform movements around the People's party. By 1896 the severe economic recession and the swallowing of the Populists by the Democratic party placed earth-shaking events like the Homestead strike, the Pullman strike, and the hunger marches on Washington into a near political vacuum. The small Socialist Labor party, loudly insisting that Revolution was around the corner, sought to take over the AFL but only destroyed itself. The hero of the Pullman strike, Eugene Debs, tried to lead his supporters toward the establishment of a utopian colony in the West, but he soon realized it was impossible to create a socialist commonwealth within capitalism. Instead, he joined with others to call for an alternative to further drift and confusion: a diverse, democratic Socialist movement.

With their constituency of immigrants and native born, city workers, small middle-class and farmers, the Socialists united in 1901 upon the grandest agitational campaign the American left had ever seen. Using electoral activity as a lever of political education, the Socialist party sent hundreds of speakers far and wide, issued millions of propaganda leaflets, and formed an umbrella beneath which state and local Socialists could adapt their message to conditions and prevailing consciousness.

From the weekly *Appeal to Reason* out of Girard, Kansas, which sometimes had pressruns of up to a million, to the Yiddish-language *Jewish Daily Forward,* the most widely circulated Yiddish-language newspaper in the world, to the scores of local sheets, Socialist views could be found in nearly every language and among any factory or village population.

Most of all, Socialists spoke for and to labor. They observed the rise of corporate might demoralizing the AFL craft worker with his proud traditions, degrading to almost unspeakable conditions the unorganized, unskilled, often foreign-born worker. Everywhere they possessed influence, they held up the beacon of labor's potential power and dignity, its need to unite against common oppressors, and its destiny to rebuild the social order.

Among important sectors of workers they gained an enthusiastic following. They brought under their banner native-born small-town workers, miners, lumberjacks, tenant farmers, railroad men, and petty merchants who saw capitalism destroying the old American ideals and who accepted the Socialists as proper successors to Tom Paine and Abe Lincoln. They also helped make a New World home for German, Jewish, Finnish, Italian, and Slavic immigrants, among others, touched by labor and radical ideas in the old country.

ACCOMPLISHMENTS

During the second decade of the century the Socialists elected hundreds of local officials in virtually every state outside the deep South, carrying the Socialist message into state legislatures and Congress. Once in office, they provided honest government and improved services—what the cynics called "sewer socialism." And they took a strong stand in support of industrial unionism, woman suffrage, and other important reform causes of the day. Sometimes they personally escorted Pinkertons and scabs out of town; almost always they would guarantee a "fair fight" instead of the police intimidation that strikers customarily faced.

But the Socialists could not build the permanent, large-scale political movement created by the contemporary European left. In the United States, the rules of the political game changed swiftly and subtly. Also, the working class that Socialists had begun to reach remained divided into dozens of discrete ethnic and geographic sectors, unintegrated for the most part into electoral politics and mobilized effectively in the first instance for better wages and conditions. And World War I threw confusion and oppression across the movement.

LIMITS

The limits of Socialist potential were first pointed up by the resurgence of reform politics. Socialists who had believed that all reactionaries would line up in the Republican party, and that the petit-bourgeois Democratic party would wither away, by 1912 confronted a multitude of local and national "progressive" reformers, symbolically led by Theodore Roosevelt's Bull Moose campaign for president. The approach of world war placed new weapons in the hands of their political enemies.

While profits boomed, politicians could arrange for important reforms, while "patriotically" supporting the suppression of Socialists and labor radicals in the courts and by vigilante squads. They could even offer AFL unions limited sanction to organize—if they would disown Socialist ideas and support the war. AFL leaders caved in; local Socialist officials lost to "fusion" and "good government" tickets set up by the major parties, while many radicals muted their dissent to stay out of prison.

Neither did Socialists find the means to relate decisively the record-breaking strike wave of 1915–19 to a political strategy. Strikers willing to fight for their lives on picket lines did not necessarily view electoral politics as a viable addition to their arsenal. "The economic theories of Socialism have found a welcome on a good many door mats, since the War," a radical union journalist wrote in 1919, "but the political phase of Socialism has become a joke in America." This was an overstatement. But certainly politics, even with a modest resurgence of local Socialist success in 1917–20, could not keep pace with the drama of labor events culminating in the national steel strike and the Seattle general strike of 1919.

INDUSTRIAL RADICALISM

Pressures upon the Socialist party, without and within, finally proved too great. At the call of the Russian Bolsheviks for a new International, Socialists fell upon each other in fratricidal conflict. Feuds, splits, and expulsions with the national "Red Scare" drove away much of the rank and file while convincing many Americans that Socialists and Communists constituted a wild and exotic political species. Long-standing supporters emerged from the maelstrom tired and often disillusioned.

Even had a powerful Socialist movement entered the postwar era intact, it would have confronted serious difficulties. American capitalism, now the strongest in the world, rolled back labor's wartime victories. Dissident movements like the regional farmer-labor parties, the ethnic labor activists, and the black militant following of Marcus Garvey seemed destined to go their separate ways.

The influence of the federal government in state and local matters as demonstrated during World War I, the increasing power of corporate financing over political campaigns, and a multitude of other factors brought the underlying assumptions of Socialist electoral tactics into question. The decision of Communists to follow labor into the New Deal coalition of Franklin D. Roosevelt's Democratic party of the mid–1930s pointed up an alternative (with its own dilemmas) that Socialists had never envisioned. The goal of radical education, from economics to culture, would have to be pursued in very different ways.

The Industrial Workers of the World supplied a key to this political enigma. Part of the answer could not be formulated until the New Deal's creation of a welfare state permitted a strategy that recognized certain structural reforms within capitalism as politically necessary for the left to demand and seek to extend. Socialists could not stand outside the immediate prospects for social security and subsequent welfare legislation of collective bargaining, civil rights enforcement, or protection of the natural environment. But neither could the labor movement and its allies succeed within the existing political rules.

The parliamentary left had never viewed the factory as the central locus of change. Socialist leaders, to say nothing of major party reform politicians, repeatedly informed labor that workplace organization was at best defensive, a holding action suited to maintain living standards while political change brought a better order. Labor struggles that united large sections of communities—not only workers in the struck industries, but also their relatives and neighbors, small business people, occasional church and synagogue officials—had, since the nineteenth century, often proved that collective action was the only effective means at hand. Labor could "vote" with its arms, legs, and mind between elections.

Through the Industrial Workers of the World, lessons of European anarchism and syndicalism merged with the practical conclusions drawn by American activists who favored direct action. The mobilization of the politically apathetic or disfranchised (youth, noncitizens, the semiliterate) to gain control over their lives tapped energies otherwise inaccessible. Aroused, with fire in their eyes, the "slaves" could be turned into freedom fighters ready to perish for the cause. Many could be converted to this new gospel by the vision of a society in which workers and others governed themselves through workshop and neighborhood units. The people of the new society would act not through politicians, however enlightened, but via direct democracy, bypassing and abolishing the coercive state. Then—in the spirit of eighteenth-century Enlightenment thought updated to the proletarian revolution—Art and Love would be free and untrammeled, life a picturesque and joyful adventure for all. However elusive such a goal, however apparently aesthetic, it appealed to many a self-taught workingman and woman, to middle-class rebels who hoped for a drastic overturn of conventional morals, to idealists disillusioned with Socialist and labor day-to-day politics.

The IWW proclaimed from its formation in 1905 the need for "One Big Union," an industrial organization of all workers rather than the fragmented and often uncooperative AFL internationals. Western miners joined by brewery workers, dozens of local and regional groups, declared themselves at the founding convention the "Continental Congress of the Working Class." With an almost religious zeal, they set out to organize the broad mass of unorganized workers across craft, race, ethnic, and sex lines. But the IWW faced severe opposition from most existing unions, lacked the financial reserves required for large-scale organization, and soon fell prey to internal squabbles. By the recession of 1907, the IWW had practically ceased to exist as a viable organization. The five or six thousand members nevertheless had an important message for labor and possessed the spirit to put that message forward. Workers had to preach solidarity even while their unions crossed each other's picket lines; they had to try out new methods of gaining solidarity, from the songs they sang to the occupation of factories. Above all, they had to confront anti-labor attacks along political, religious, ethnic, racial or so-called moral lines with their own standards. Labor had to cease begging for favors and proclaim its ability to produce and distribute goods without the interference of the profit system.

When electrical workers in Schenectady, New York, sat down at their jobs in 1908, they announced through the IWW not properly a "protest" but a *claim upon labor's rightful due.* The skilled worker had a centurys-old feeling of pride in craftsmanship and relative power over production. But without the proper sentiment, this power might be exercised undemocratically, considered the prerogative of only the best-paid strata. The IWW brought the idea that, when industrial production becomes socialized, the combination of many machines and skills, the range of potential cooperation and industrial democracy, extended to everyone on the floor.

The labor upsurge after 1910, mobilizing millions of previously unorganized workers for gains that had been decades in the making, gave these ideals a vast popularity. The IWW itself drew special devotion from two kinds of workers. The foreign-born toilers from eastern and southern Europe—Italians, Slavs, Hungarians, and others, along with the Finns—often heard the call for industrial unionism first from the IWW, and they received reassurance that they, more than the rich idlers, constituted the real America. The IWW also appealed to those workers cut off from most home and family ties—the "timber wolves" of southern lumber, "bindle stiffs" of agricultural production in the West, loggers, seamen, and others who found in the Wobblies an alternative to the bars, company towns, flophouses, and Salvation Army halls. The IWW agitator, who spoke several tongues and customarily risked life and limb in order to preach the message, became for these workers and others an almost legendary figure. With his "Little Red Book" of IWW songs "To Fan the Flames of Discontent," his pamphlets and newspapers to sell or give away, his faith in workers' power, he offered living proof that the labor movement stood on new ground.

The Lawrence, Massachusetts, textile strike of 1912 stood as that proof like no previous event. Slavs, Italians, Irish, Greeks— two dozen language groups in all—went out to fight mill owners who reduced wages in accordance with the statutory reduction of the work week to 56 hours. The IWW brought in its great personalities: "Big Bill" Haywood, former leader of the western miners and founder of the IWW; Arturo Giovannitti, labor's most famous poet and leader of the Italian radicals; Elizabeth Gurley Flynn, the "Rebel Girl" still in her teens but already known as a great female orator. The movement also organized soup kitchens and clothing distribution, and even arranged for the strikers' children to be sent to other cities for the duration of the conflict. When the hostile press roared at the impudence of and "danger" posed by these ragged immigrant workers who resisted employers, police, and AFL craft unions alike, IWW militants named the strike a "trial of a new civilization." And so it was. The strikers won clean on the issue of hours, and if they did not gain a union contract, there was at least a significant improvement in their condition and an immeasurable moral triumph. For more than a year the excitement ran up and down the east coast, drawing Italian immigrant workers and others into numerous hard-fought struggles that promised to usher in a new era for labor.

During this historic upsurge artists, many intellectuals, feminists, and others also looked to the IWW for cultural leadership of the masses. Wobbly songwriters such as Joe Hill penned ballads of workers' courage, satires upon contemporary religious melodies, ferocious cries of determination to overwhelm an oppressive social system. Across the world these songs became popular in labor and radical movements. Poetry also thundered out from IWW and related publications, including the weekly Italian-language *Il Proletario* with the outstanding lyric rebel of the day, Arturo Giovannitti, at its helm. Many IWW leaders and activists joined Margaret Sanger in distribution of birth control information that was then illegal and dangerous to possess. Truly, the IWW thought itself nearing that new civilization.

The IWW could not sustain its momentum against the overwhelming odds. The Catholic church joined businessmen and many local labor officials in branding the organization atheistic and un-American. Impoverished strikers lacked the resources for lengthy battles. In Paterson, New Jersey, in Akron, Ohio, and in dozens of other cities large and small the pounding pressure of police violence and the slow starvation of resources killed the strikes by degrees. Pushed back to the West, virtually driven underground by savage legal repression and vigilante action during World War I, the IWW lost out to a new and different labor tendency. Important IWW leaders along with many thousand followers joined the AFL or independent unions founded or rejuvenated during the war, when better economic conditions and a tightened labor market at last brought skilled and unskilled together into the mainstream. The new unions lacked, for the most part, the IWW's ideological stridency. But they could deliver, and hold on.

Still, the IWW influence had not been wholly spent. On the Philadelphia docks the Wobblies showed how interracial unionism could benefit all workers. They organized farm workers, joining with Mexican-American activists decades before Cesar Chavez and his movement went to the fields. They were the first to invade Henry Ford's Detroit factories, bringing the mass production workers at the center of future industrial unionism the message that labor power at the point of production held the secret of collective advance. Although they might have failed to organize permanent bodies, although they might decline to a minuscule propaganda group, the Wobblies had nevertheless placed their stamp upon American labor's future. Two decades later the labor mainstream called the higher "politics" of factory-floor direct action the CIO.

Other lessons kept the IWW a romantic legend decades afterward. Because it had been so fervently egalitarian, so devoted to the bottommost layers of productive labor, it pointed to the essentially *moral* quality of all labor movements at their best. Some promise of freedom breathed in the nineteenth century, unrealized in either class-divided East or West, remained at the core of labor's appeal. Higher wages, better conditions, a good union contract alone—no self-respecting Wobbly would consider these adequate accomplishments. The vision of self-rule, of a free people charting their own destiny, remained alive so long as a single American worker refused to accept the status of slave to an alarm clock and a bankbook.

STRIKE NOTICE

To All Pullman Porters and Maids

On account of the refusal of the Pullman Company to settle the dispute on Recognition of Wages and Rules governing Working Conditions with the Brotherhood of Sleeping Car Porters, a strike has been declared and shall be enforced on all Pullman Cars effective

FRIDAY, JUNE 8th
12 O'clock Noon

For further information call Glendale **6373.** You are requested to attend the meetings to be held each evening from 4 until 6 o'clock at **2382 18th street.**

BENNIE SMITH
Field Organizer

By Order of Strike Committee

Strike notice for the Brotherhood of Sleeping Car Porters, Detroit, June 7, 1928. From Schnapper, *American Labor*.

Black Workers from Reconstruction to the Great Depression

Nell Irvin Painter

Black workers' relationship to unions and labor politics is closely tied to black participation in politics, their minority status in nearly all occupations, and the race prejudice of white workers. Between 1865 and 1941 the record is pretty dismal. Until the late 1930s, when hundreds of thousands of Negroes had migrated from the South to the North, where they could vote and exercise political power, and when the new unions of the Congress of Industrial Organizations (CIO) began including them, black workers lacked effective voices in their workplaces and in the political arena.

The era of exclusion may now have passed forever from the labor scene. As long as Afro-Americans wield enough political clout to insure fair employment practices, labor will not easily return to the racist practices of the past. Yet as long as unemployment remains disproportionate, jobless black workers, particularly young people, provide a labor pool that threatens the achievements of organized labor in wages, work safety, and job security. It is possible that an anti-union administration in Washington may buy the allegiance of Negroes with low-paying non-union jobs, reopening a racial breach in the workforce that would be detrimental to all of labor.

AFTER SLAVERY

A. Philip Randolph, the most prominent black unionist, noted that "the labor movement cannot afford to be split along any lines." That sentiment has been honored in words, at least, by nearly every federation of labor—if not by individual locals and unions or on the shop floor—from the time of the earliest post-Civil War labor organizations.

Between 1866 and the early 1870s the National Labor Union gave occasional lip service to the idea of organizing Negroes, but partisan politics and racial antipathy frustrated any meaningful action. Meanwhile, blacks organized their own union, the Colored National Labor Union, which lasted from 1869 to 1874 in the Washington area. This organization exemplified much that has typified black political activity from before the Civil War to the present time, for though nearly every Negro, male and female, works for a living, black leaders are not noted for their working-class demeanor. If anything, outstanding blacks have tended more to resemble gentlemen than workingmen.

Accordingly, many of the figures prominent in the Colored National Labor Union were not workers but race spokesmen, journalists and politicians such as Frederick Douglass, Henry Highland Garnet, and John Mercer Langston. But each of these men had worked hard as a youngster, and they shared a concern for the working-class interests of blacks that only a union could address. They also agreed that the Republican party best represented their interests as a race.

In the South, where most blacks lived until the 1960s, the Republican party in the late 1860s and early 1870s was the party of working people. In a region where the great majority farmed, land tenure and credit practices were prime concerns. To the extent that either party represented working-class interests in the heyday of black voting (1867–76), the Republican party stood for its constituency of newly enfranchised blacks. In the best of conditions, as in Louisiana or South Carolina, Republicans in southern legislatures championed free public schools, land reform, and exemption laws (which placed personal property beyond the reach of foreclosure when a crop did not pay the landowner's or shopkeeper's share or rent). This identification of the Republican party with black interests outlived racial and economic realities, moving one black journalist to note, in 1918, the absurdity of "a race of tenants and workers accepting political leaders selected by landlords, bankers and big capitalists."

THE KNIGHTS OF LABOR

The great labor movement of the late nineteenth century was the Knights of Labor. Begun in the late 1860s in Pennsylvania, it peaked in 1886 with more than 700,000 members. Taking the entire American working class, skilled and unskilled, as its constituency, the Knights hoped eventually to replace the wage system with a cooperative commonwealth encompassing all Americans regardless of sex or color. In the interim, however, the Knights' power translated into a wave of strikes that crested in 1886, the year of labor's great upheaval.

The most extensive of the year's 1,400 strikes spread across Texas, Kansas, Nebraska, Missouri, and Arkansas as the Knights of Labor struck the Gould railroad system in what came to be known as the Great Southwestern Strike. The grievances of black workers lay at its center. The strike, which was ultimately lost, aimed to secure recognition of the Knights and to raise the wages of unskilled, poorly paid sectionmen, many of whom were black. Unlike the newly organized American Federation of Labor (AFL), the Knights of Labor embraced unskilled workers. At that time some 60,000 Knights were black, and black women made up several local assemblies—laundresses, domestic workers, and especially tobacco workers around Richmond, Virginia.

In 1886 the Knights of Labor was strong enough in Richmond to host the union's largest annual convention. But Richmond's southern mores provoked an incident that centered on a well-known Negro Knight, Frank Ferrell of New York City's outspoken District Assembly 49. When a Richmond hotelkeeper drew the color line against Ferrell, his white brothers joined him in lodgings in the Negro section of town. And in the convention's opening session Ferrell introduced Terence Powderly, the Grand Master Workman, with a ringing denunciation of racial discrimination.

The outcome pleased black workers but alienated southern white Knights, whose idea of appropriate union activity inclined less toward social reform than toward the pure and simple unionism of the AFL. As the Knights declined in the following years, the AFL shunned wider reforms for the most part and stuck to narrow, achievable aims.

This is not to say that in its early years the AFL did not speak and act occasionally to discourage racial proscription in its affiliated unions. When in the late 1880s the International Association of Machinists barred black workers, the AFL encouraged the organization of a rival union. Throughout the 1880s and most of the 1890s, the Federation spoke bravely of a union movement of all American workers regardless of color. In action, however, it was far less vigorous.

THE PEOPLE'S PARTY

Spurned by the two major parties, many workers and farmers took part in the People's party, which grew out of a coalition of unions and farmers' alliances of the South and West. At the organizing meeting for the third party in 1891, Terence Powderly of the Knights of Labor and Ignatius Donnelly of the western Farmers' Alliance denounced sectionalism and the color line in politics. The People's party, they promised, would unite the producers of the South and West, farmers and workmen, black and white. Although the white southern Farmers' Alliance was militant on farm issues, it held back from the third-party movement because of the race issue. They had not objected to a separate Colored Farmers' Alliance so long as it did not show any great independence of action, but in the late 1880s and early 1890s the Colored Alliance offended the racial attitudes of white Alliancemen.

In 1889 in Mississippi, Colored Alliancemen boycotted white merchants who overcharged, a tactic Alliancemen had often used to good effect. But when the governor sent in the militia and several black Alliancemen were killed, their white counterparts kept silent. When the Colored Alliance supported the Lodge federal elections bill of 1890, which would have safeguarded black suffrage, white Alliancemen opposed the Colored Alliance. Finally, the Colored Alliance organized a strike of agricultural workers (cotton pickers) in 1891—which the white Alliancemen broke, in their role of employers. There was to be no cooperation of southern producers across the color line in the late nineteenth century.

The most potent enemy of third-party politics in the South was the whites' fear of black political power, even when exercised in the interest of producer unity. There were some exceptions, such as Leonidas L. Polk of North Carolina and Tom Watson of Georgia, but for most southern whites the conviction that government was the preserve of white men overrode any sentiments of interracial class solidarity, on the land or in the shop.

AMERICAN SEPARATION OF LABOR

By the turn of the century, racial exclusion and segregation were becoming law, not just custom. By 1910 all southern states had virtually eliminated black voting through grandfather clauses or poll taxes. The pure and simple craft unionism of the AFL no longer challenged the color line in its unions or political parties. Racial exclusion was the rule in both places in the early twentieth century.

With the exception of the mineworkers' and longshoremen's unions, the left-led unions, and the unique Brotherhood of Sleeping Car Porters, black workers and organized labor were mutually exclusive until the rise of the CIO in the mid-1930s. In East St. Louis in 1917 and in Chicago in 1919, the combination of strikes and racially split workforces sparked anti-black pogroms. Although violent upheavals on the order of Chicago and East St. Louis were unusual, such conditions occurred time and again in industrial centers: unions excluded blacks, factories ordinarily did not employ blacks, but when white workers went out on strike, black workers—sometimes brought in from the South—got jobs as strikebreakers. To many white union men, a black man was naturally a scab.

Afro-Americans were divided and understandably ambivalent about organized labor in the nineteenth and early twentieth centuries. Reformers associated with white philanthropists, such as Booker T. Washington of Tuskegee Institute, played down the importance of unionization. But younger blacks recognized that Negroes needed unions as much as any other working-class group and that this natural leaning was frustrated only by racism in the labor movement. A. Philip Randolph, editor of the New York *Messenger,* called the AFL the "American Separation of Labor" and labeled it "the most wicked machine for the propagation of race prejudice in the country."

In fact, the AFL seemed bent on living up to Randolph's characterization in the first third of this century. When W. E. B. Du Bois and other blacks in the Niagara movement called for entry of blacks into unions in 1905, the AFL was not listening. During the vicious campaign waged by the railroad brotherhoods to oust Negroes from skilled jobs in that industry, the AFL registered no protest. And when the National Association for the Advancement of Colored People called for the formation of an interracial labor commission in the mid-1920s, Samuel Gompers and the Federation made no response.

Exceptions occurred only where blacks constituted a significant proportion of the workforce, as among longshoremen in coastal ports and in the industries clustered around Birmingham, Alabama, where half the miners and 65 percent of the iron- and steelworkers were Negroes. There an integrated labor movement flourished between 1894 and 1904. Operators broke both a series of strikes and the interracial unions by importing white workers from the North. But for a time at least, Birmingham's workers realized their full strength through interracial organization.

The only predominantly white AFL union with significant Negro membership was the United Mine Workers, formed in

1890, from the beginning a partially industrial union. In 1902 the mineworkers represented 20,000 Negro miners, or half the total blacks in the AFL. The UMW organized black miners in Ohio, Kentucky, West Virginia, Pennsylvania, and Alabama. It was fortunate both for the industrial union movement and for Afro-American workers that the impetus for the CIO came largely from the UMW, where blacks came closest to sharing equally in the union. The miners compiled a record for organizing black workers that was approached only by the small and marginal organizations on the left: the Industrial Workers of the World, the Western Federation of Miners (later the Mine, Mill and Smelter Workers Union), and the unions associated with the Communist party—the Trade Union Educational League, the Trade Union Unity League, and the American Negro Labor Congress.

THE BROTHERHOOD

This country's only predominantly black union was organized in 1925, when a group of Pullman porters approached the socialist journalist A. Philip Randolph. They belonged to a company union that they felt did not adequately represent them. Other porters had attempted to organize in 1900, 1912, and 1924, but without lasting success.

The Brotherhood of Sleeping Car Porters struggled for four years before receiving any recognition from the AFL and for a dozen years before being recognized by the Pullman Company. The Hotel and Restaurant Employees Alliance blocked the Brotherhood's application for affiliation with the AFL in 1926 on the grounds that the porters were more waiters than railroad workers. Yet the hotel and restaurant workers had made no attempt to organize the Pullman porters; indeed, their constitution barred black members. The hotel workers preferred to organize segregated auxiliaries for the porters. In 1928 the AFL accepted the Brotherhood as a group of affiliated locals and granted full international status in 1936.

In 1937 the Pullman Company recognized the Brotherhood in

the first agreement ever signed between a Negro union and a major employer. The agreement provided for higher wages and the abolition of unpaid work and excessive working hours. Between 1926 and 1937 the company had denied the Brotherhood recognition by firing porters active in the union and replacing them with Filipino workers, and by contending that porters were not railroad workers and hence unaffected by the Railway Labor Act of 1926, which provided for union representation.

For Afro-Americans the Brotherhood was more than simply a union of Pullman porters. It stood for black labor in general. A. Philip Randolph, head of the union, came to be known as Mr. Black Labor, the most prominent spokesman for black workers within or without his or other unions. Black people of all sorts respected Randolph and the Brotherhood as the appropriate representative of the race.

Serious opposition came, rather, from the left. Radical criticism had begun as soon as the Brotherhood applied for affiliation with the AFL, when the American Negro Labor Congress criticized Randolph for selling out and forsaking "militant struggle in the interest of the workers for the policy of class collaboration with the bosses." The opposition of the ANLC, which never reached large numbers of black workers, was not as painful for Randolph as his break with the much larger National Negro Congress in 1940.

Randolph had been anti-Communist for decades when, as president of the National Negro Congress, he criticized the Soviet Union in a speech. The Congress voted him out of office and elected a former YMCA secretary who was closer to Communist party policies. This move, in connection with several other NNC actions that accorded closely with Communist party positions, made many blacks see the Congress as less of a black organization and more of an appendage of the Communist party. Randolph regretted his ouster from a national Afro-American organization, but the action did not prevent him from influencing federal employment policies.

FAIR EMPLOYMENT PRACTICES

The oldest grievance of black workers in this country has been exclusion from employment. When the United States geared up for defense production in 1940, black workers were routinely refused employment, even when they possessed valuable skills. The federal government awarded the contracts and paid the bills, but it did not enforce clauses that barred racial discrimination in war work. The existence of such clauses testified to the political clout of northern blacks, who, unlike their peers in southern states, could vote. Responding to a groundswell of black opinion, Randolph and the Brotherhood formed the March on Washington Movement to bring 100,000 Negroes to the capital in 1941 to protest discrimination in war work and the armed forces: "We loyal American citizens demand the right to work and fight for our country," said the call to action.

Faced with this threat of mass action, President Franklin D. Roosevelt signed Executive Order 8802, one of the most important victories in the black struggle for equality. It banned racial discrimination in defense industries and government employment, but not in the armed forces, which remained segregated until the mid–1950s.

Organized black labor, embodied in Randolph and the Brotherhood of Sleeping Car Porters, spearheaded the movement for fair employment that opened industrial jobs to blacks. Access to remunerative employment was the vital first step of blacks out of a netherland of poverty and into the American mainstream. By the end of World War II black workers were positioned to take their rightful places in organized labor and to pressure for legislation that furthered their own working-class interests. The New Deal coalition of blacks, liberals, and organized labor produced the legislative underpinnings of the civil rights revolution and the social welfare programs of the Great Society that have so benefited workers and poor people in this country regardless of race.

Photographs from federal relief agencies portrayed Depression hardships that lay behind Farmer-Labor movements. From Schnapper, *American Labor*.

The Farmer-Labor Party

David Montgomery

"The Republicans and Democrats both belong to big business. We need a party of our own." How often workers say that! But what is a labor party, and how would it operate within the American political framework? Between the world wars several efforts were made to create a national labor party, and the Farmer-Labor party of Minnesota became the strongest political force in the state. An examination of those efforts, and especially of the Minnesota movement, might help us to think more clearly about what a labor party could mean today and tomorrow.

The attempt to create a new political movement after World War I grew out of a strike wave that involved between one and four million workers every year, and the rapid growth of AFL unions in mass production industries such as textiles, coal, meatpacking, and railroads. Not only did the police and the army routinely attack strikers during these conflicts, but the Republican administration in Washington was publicly committed to ending inflation by deregulating corporate industry and reducing production costs through wage cuts and elimination of union work rules. Wartime experience had made the power of government over daily life evident to everyone. Consequently workers were asking why, if the world had just been saved for democracy, the "democratic" state couldn't fight on their side.

The main political agency available to workers before the war, the Socialist party, had broken into three parts. A revolutionary wing became affiliated with the Communist International. By

1922 the Communists emerged from clandestine activity and persecution as a small but influential force in Finnish, Slavic, and Jewish fraternal organizations and in the unions of garment workers, coalminers, and machinists. The Socialist party itself remained a power in Milwaukee, Reading, and some other municipalities, enjoying the friendly cooperation of many union functionaries and intellectuals. But many followers of the prewar SP had deserted their party in favor of purely electoral movements which emphasized the immediate needs of working people and proclaimed their loyalty to the government during the war. The most important of these was the Nonpartisan League.

The Nonpartisan League was created by Socialists in North Dakota who realized that the exploitation of the state's farmers by grain dealers, banks, and railroads, and the brazen success of those interests in frustrating all efforts of farmers to help themselves, had enraged innumerable lifelong Republicans. The remedy envisaged by A. C. Townley, Arthur LeSueur, and their comrades was to enter the Republican primaries with a disciplined organization of farmers and workers. The keys to their approach were local meetings at which everyone who had paid a dollar to join could help select one of their number for NPL endorsement in the primaries; a platform calling for state-owned banks, grain elevators, and other marketing agencies, to which candidates were pledged; and a disciplined caucus of elected members. The success of the movement was almost miraculous. In 1917 seventy-two of the ninety-seven Republican legislators and fifteen of the sixteen Democrats were in the NPL caucus. That caucus cut through parliamentary mysteries, allowing farmers to formulate their own bills in a setting where everyone was committed to doing what the majority decided. The 1919 session, where the NPL controlled both houses as well as Governor Lynn Frazier, was the only one in the state's history to finish its business within the constitutionally mandated sixty days, and it created a state bank, grain elevators, hail insurance, workmen's compensation, income and inheritance taxes, home buyers' assistance, restrictions on injunctions in strikes, and the country's best mine safety law. No more dramatic demonstration of democracy has occurred in American history.

The NPL's success in electing candidates pledged to its program through the primaries of North Dakota's major parties spread its influence quickly to neighboring states and to Canada. By 1920 it had 50,000 members in Minnesota and had chosen more than thirty rural legislators in each of two elections. But Minnesota was very different from North Dakota. Minneapolis was the home of the hated grain exchange; St. Paul and Duluth were manufacturing and shipping centers. The Mesabi range yielded untold wealth in iron ore to U.S. Steel through the toil of laborers who had migrated from Finland, Croatia, Italy, and the Ukraine. Moreover, even the countryside was a mosaic of immigrant nationalities and New England Yankees, and it was spotted with railroad junctions and meatpacking towns. The Republicans had long dominated the state's politics with the help of bountiful business contributions, the commercial press of the Twin Cities, and personable Scandinavian candidates. Nevertheless, the Democrats were powerful in Irish St. Paul and had almost carried the presidential election of 1916. In the same year the Socialist Thomas Van Lear was elected mayor of Minneapolis. Minnesota's political revolt, therefore, was influenced by the NPL, but assumed its own distinctive form, in which labor's role was decisive.

Both the war and the postwar depression (1920–22) brought Minnesota's farmers and workers together. Opposition to America's declaration of war had been so widespread that four of the state's nine congressmen voted against U.S. intervention. Rural Germans held mass rallies to keep the boys home. Although the NPL pledged its loyalty and called for "conscription of wealth" in order to "win our war," such open enemies of the war as Congressman Charles A. Lindbergh evoked roars of approval from NPL meetings whenever he ignored the leaders and denounced the carnage. A wartime strike of streetcar drivers brought the Twin Cities to the verge of a general strike. In response to this ferment Governor J. A. A. Burnquist established a Commission of Public Safety which fiercely persecuted dissidents, especially the NPL. During the 1918 primaries NPL meetings were banned in nineteen counties, and Townley was jailed for sedition the following year.

FROM PRIMARIES TO A PARTY

Nonpartisan leagues of farmers and workers at first functioned
separately, but their combined strength threw the Republicans
into confusion. Concessions clearly had to be made in order to
abate the popular anger, but "steel Republicans" and "grain
Republicans" fought each other over who should foot the bill.
For example, the Republican legislature passed a heavy tax on
iron mining, which the Republican governor vetoed—only to
have the Republican platform committed to it, while the steel
companies mobilized a fair tax association against it. In the
Republican primary of 1920, 39 percent of the vote went to NPL
candidates, with the rural constituencies of the league winning
elections. The labor sections introduced the ideas of public
ownership of industry, forced the movement to exchange primary campaigns for a new party, and provided the links between
that party and nationwide third-party efforts.

The NPL opposed the idea of a new party because its success
had come through primaries; the Socialist party resisted the
formation of a rival in order to hold its own votes; the Communists were then committed to combatting all "reformist"
movements. Nonetheless William Mahoney, Robley Cramer, and
other active trade unionists were convinced that the time was
ripe. Sensing how bitterly both farmers and workers had been
alienated by the Republicans' ruthless "deflation" program and
the Democrats' inability to mount a serious alternative, the
workers' league prodded the farmers into joining them in entering
a new ticket, for the Farmer-Labor party, in the 1922 elections.
Although its platform focused on labor's needs, its top candidates
were from the farm movement, and Henrik Shipstead, the
senatorial candidate, virtually ran his own campaign. That
election established the FLP as the second party of Minnesota,
sending Shipstead to the Senate and garnering about 38 percent
of the votes, as compared to 45 percent for the Republicans and
10 percent for the Democrats.

Most important of all, during the next three years the party
worked out a structure that distinguished it from the Republicans

or Democrats. It had a dues-paying membership; individuals affiliated through ward clubs, while unions and cooperatives joined as organizations with appropriate voting power. The party had its own press and educational bodies. At biannual conventions it thrashed out policies that were binding on its candidates. Women were prominent in the FLP, though there was a noticeable change between the 1920s, when women were always included among the candidates for top state offices, and the 1930s, when they never were. State committee members such as Susie Stageberg, Marian LeSueur, and Selma Seestrom played major policymaking roles. One thing the party could always count on was huge voter turnouts. During the 1920s, when nationwide voter participation fell below 50 percent, between 90 and 95 percent of the eligible voters came to the polls in every Minnesota election.

Efforts to form a national party during these years failed. The heart of the problem was that labor unions in basic industries were virtually wiped out during the 1920–22 depression, and those unions had been the base of progressive policies in the AFL. In 1922 the railroad brotherhoods and the unions for coalminers, machinists, and the needle trades had formed a Conference for Progressive Political Action to promote public ownership of railroads and mines and to elect friends of labor to Congress. Few of its leaders had favored a new party, however. By early 1924, when the FLP invited labor and other organizations all over the country to send delegates to St. Paul for a national third party, Samuel Gompers and other AFL leaders were fiercely attacking all advocates of such ideas within their ranks, and the CPPA was hanging its hopes on a presidential campaign by Robert M. LaFollette. But though LaFollette supported labor's political demands, he denounced the idea of a labor party. The American way, said he, was to run as an independent individual, not to form a "class party." His repudiation of the St. Paul convention kept most potential delegates away and left Mahoney and the Communists locked in a bitter battle for the leadership of those who remained. The national party died quickly. LaFollette went to the voters as an independent, and he won far fewer votes in Minnesota than did the FLP candidate for governor.

Although the FLP's support stagnated at 20–25 percent of the voters during the "Coolidge prosperity" and was sustained mainly in impoverished farmers and beleaguered trade unionists, the coming of the Great Depression gave new strength and direction to both the state and national movements. The League for Independent Political Action, formed in 1928 by such people as Mahoney, John Dewey, W. E. B. Du Bois, J. B. S. Hardman, and Paul Douglas, provided the main organizing force in the campaign for a new labor party. By 1935 LIPA's efforts had helped produce demands for a new party from hundreds of city and state labor bodies, the international unions of railroad, textile, and needle trades workers, and half a dozen congressmen, including Vito Marcantonio and Robert M. LaFollette, Jr. Nevertheless, these hopes collapsed in 1936 as abruptly as had those of 1924. Labor's Nonpartisan Political League (formed by the emerging CIO) threw all its weight behind Roosevelt, who was campaigning for reelection, and the Socialists decided to run their own presidential campaign. The movement's desertion by these indispensable forces left the remaining LIPA activists afraid that their proposed party would be controlled by the Communists, who strongly supported the movement. To avoid this outcome LIPA scuttled its own anticlimactic convention in May 1936, passing a resolution that turned the whole matter of forming a new party over to the Minnesota Farmer-Labor party. The Minnesotans, then fighting for their political lives, were in no position to spearhead a nationwide movement in defiance of Franklin Roosevelt's Democrats.

TO THE COOPERATIVE COMMONWEALTH

The FLP rode to power in Minnesota on a wave of popular struggles. The Farm Holiday Association blockaded market deliveries of milk and produce and obstructed sheriff sales of foreclosed farms in 1932 and 1933. Striking truckdrivers, packing-house workers, knitwear and metal fabricating workers, and iron miners battled police and goons to break the open-shop grip of business's Citizens' Alliance. A people's lobby numbering tens of thousands descended on the capitol in 1934 to push unemployment compensation and a farm mortgage moratorium through the Republican-controlled state senate. In this setting Floyd Olson, the FLP's most popular figure, won the governorship with 57 percent of the votes in 1930 and was re-elected in 1932 and 1934.

Being in office during the worst years of a Depression did not lead to defeat for the FLP, as it so often did for other parties. True, the press and many voters blamed the violent struggles of 1933–34 on the FLP, but those actions also resulted in stronger labor support and the radicalization of Olson and the party's platform. The 1934 convention did not simply echo the New Deal but called instead for "immediate steps . . . to abolish capitalism in a peaceful and lawful manner." Idle plants were to be commandeered by the state to make jobs for the unemployed, and the state government was called upon to take possession of all factories, mines, and utilities, except those that were already cooperatively owned.

During the next four years business's hostility toward the FLP reached a fever pitch. Courts and legislatures, radio, press, and pulpit were theaters of unending confrontations. Nevertheless, the rapid growth of the union movement solidified the working-class vote to such an extent that in 1936 Elmer Benson won a record 58 percent of the votes for governor, five of the nine congressmen were FLP, and the party had 50,000 dues-paying members and 100,000 subscribers to its paper. A critical weakness, however, lay in the division of the labor movement on which the party was based. The AFL fought the rising CIO both in the factories and inside the councils of the FLP. Special ideological intensity was injected into the conflict by the fact that the Communists were strong in the CIO while the Trotskyists were powerful in the AFL (through their leadership of the local teamsters). The AFL fiercely opposed Communist efforts to build a popular front through the FLP and the CIO; it staged a mass rally on April 11, 1938, featuring Trotskyite speakers who opposed any form of unity with Stalinists. These divisions led the AFL forces to embrace Mayor Latimer of Minneapolis, despite his record of personally leading scabs across picket lines, when the latter led anti-Communist moves in the FLP and shrewdly lent his name to the international defense of Trotsky.

DEFEAT AND FUSION

The FLP's year of decision came in 1938. As the Great Depression wallowed in its second downturn, Republican strength increased sharply all over the country. Conservatives in Minnesota logjammed the FLP's legislative program, while the commercial press attacked it relentlessly. Hjalmar Peterson, Governor Benson's frustrated rival for the FLP nomination, waged a two-year campaign against the incumbent's leadership, which became increasingly anti-Semitic. Republicans picked up the theme, and by election day the state had been decked out in billboards portraying "Jewish Red conspirators" dominating the FLP and riding roughshod over the various nationalities of hard-working taxpayers. Mailboxes were stuffed with copies of Ray Chase's infamous pamphlet about the FLP, *Are They Communists or Catspaws?* While President Roosevelt ignored Benson's pleas for help, congressman Martin Dies brought his new House Un-American Activities Committee to Minnesota for an investigation.

Harold Stassen, running on the Republican ticket with promises to administer a New Deal–type program for the state while barring the gates against Reds and Revolution, won 59 percent of the votes; Benson received 34 percent. Moreover, in a desperate effort to weather the storm, the FLP had beaten a programmatic retreat at its 1938 convention, virtually cleansing the party's public posture of all traces of socialism. This was more than a defeat: it was a rout. By 1940 the party's membership had fallen to 4,000. So bitter were the movement's internal divisions that, when Hjalmar Peterson did win the FLP's gubernatorial nomination in 1942, the CIO endorsed Stassen. Major party leaders were trying to purge alleged Communists from the ranks and effect a merger with the Democrats. National figures associated with LIPA followed the same course, and virtually all devoted their efforts after 1938 to reelecting Roosevelt and mobilizing support for his foreign policy.

The end of the FLP came in 1944, when its left-wing leaders joined the merger movement in the name of unity in the war against fascism and the "spirit of Teheran." The master of ceremonies at the celebration of the merger was Hubert H. Humphrey, the rising young star of the Democrats. Four years later, when the leadership of the Democratic-Farmer-Labor party supported Henry Wallace for president, Hunphrey would lead the purge that brought the party in line for Harry Truman and the Cold War.

The Republicans and Democrats had snuffed out an open worker- and farmer-based party run by dues-paying members and with a program committed to public ownership and production for use. Before its demise the party won many elections, infused the state with a progressive political atmosphere that is still evident, and revealed that it is possible in America to engage in politics for socialism.

While the FLP provides a useful guide to future action, it also leaves us with major questions to consider. What new social groupings such as Chicanos, feminists, consumer and energy groups, must be involved in organizing socialist politics today? How should mass parties and Marxist-Leninist vanguard parties relate to each other? Is it wise to trim the socialist sails in the face of attack, as the FLP did in 1938, or might a defeat with flags held high have kept alive a mass socialist base from which to launch the next round of struggle? How do we move a labor party today beyond the realm of resolutions? These questions will have to be thrashed out in real life, if we are to live up to the legacy of Minnesota's workers and farmers.

The Memorial Day massacre, Republic Steel, Chicago, 1937. From Schnapper, *American Labor*.

Labor and the New Deal

James R. Green

The 1930s were heroic years for the labor movement. The Congress of Industrial Organizations exploded onto the scene when millions of hitherto unorganized production workers mobilized against their employers. Unions won a major victory with the Wagner Act, which created the National Labor Relations Board to supervise union elections and collective bargaining. Decades of neglect of social welfare ended with such New Deal legislation as social security, progressive taxation, and work relief.

These measures were labor's gateway to the New Deal coalitions. Most labor leaders, including most CIO officials and many former socialists, sacrificed political independence to enter the Democratic party. Although parties on the left vied with the Democrats in state and local elections, enthusiasm for a third party faded after Franklin D. Roosevelt's triumphant election to a second term in 1936.

There were obvious gains from entering the New Deal coalition, but what were the losses? The pressures to work inside the Democratic party proved irresistible to organized labor, but worker insurgency had developed outside it. Did these movements provide the basis for an independent political movement?

Ever since the formation of the New Deal coalition, most big unions (like the United Auto Workers) have become dependent upon the Democrats. Their leaders have come to fear the kind of rank-and-file insurgency that would be necessary for any viable third party. This has been the case at least since 1936, when labor's Non-Partisan League was formed, in part, to head off left alternatives to the Democrats at the state and local levels. In 1935 these forces won a respectable minority for a National Farmer-Labor party at the American Federation of Labor's national convention, but nothing came of the effort. Understanding why a farmer-labor party did not form then may help us to understand the dilemma that working-class voters find themselves confronting today.

LEGACY OF THE 1920s

The working-class movement entered the Great Depression with enormous liabilities. The AFL had lost about two million members during the 1920s as a result of depression, unemployment, attacks by open-shop employers, hostile legislation, and anti-union injunctions. The Socialist party, once influential in the AFL, had collapsed as a result of wartime suppression and the Communist split in 1919. The Communist party engaged in militant strike activity in the 1920s, but it was still a relatively isolated sect when the Depression hit.

Except for a brief flirtation with Senator LaFollette's 1924 Progressive campaign for president, the AFL maintained its old policy of rewarding friends and punishing enemies, and it used its influence to quash further labor party efforts. The AFL's "nonpartisanship" in national elections so limited its influence that FDR virtually ignored unions in his 1932 presidential campaign. In retrospect, it is clear that unions came to depend too much on state protection during the New Deal; but at the onset of the Depression the AFL "nonpartisan" philosophy was a weakness, not a strength.

During the first hundred days of the New Deal, Congress enacted a spate of reforms, including protection legislation opposed by the AFL. The National Recovery Act (NRA) gave mild encouragement to collective bargaining under section 7(a) and included codes pointing toward minimum wages and maximum hours. Given the way big business used the NRA for its own ends, AFL opposition was understandable. By opting out of the initial struggle in the political arena, however, the unions left labor and social legislation largely in the hands of Democratic politicians, not all of them friendly to labor, and to New Deal bureaucrats, many of them social workers. In other words, organized labor had no real program to meet the Depression crisis and found itself largely on the defensive during the first years of the New Deal.

REVOLT AGAINST NRA, 1933–35

Not all AFL leaders ignored the pro-labor potential of the NRA. Industrial unions had always been more active than craft unions in seeking state intervention. David Dubinsky of the International Ladies Garment Workers and Sidney Hillman of the Amalgamated Clothing Workers were former socialists who believed in the need for state regulation in their chaotic, depressed industries. John L. Lewis, head of the United Mine Workers, though nominally a Republican, also used the NRA to his advantage. All three industrial unions took advantage of the NRA and the disarray of the employers to reorganize themselves in 1933.

In general, though, industrial workers gained little under the NRA and often suffered setbacks. Many employers used the act to form company unions. The Communist and Socialist parties attacked the NRA as a semi-fascist attempt to save big business through state intervention. While the left attacked the "National Run Around," it also mobilized an effective unemployed workers' movement in many cities. The militant tactics adopted by left-led unemployed councils helped force the Roosevelt administration to enact direct relief.

Popular electoral movements such as Huey Long's "Share the Wealth" clubs and Upton Sinclair's "End Poverty in California" campaign for governor operated to the left of the New Deal within the Democratic party. On the outside socialists won municipal victories in Bridgeport and Milwaukee, and Floyd

Olson won election as governor of Minnesota on a farmer-labor ticket. In some industrial cities, labor party sentiment resurfaced for the first time in a decade. While the Socialist party adopted a flexible attitude toward farmer-labor parties, the Communists at first opposed reform activity of any kind.

Working-class militancy exploded across the country in 1934, when 1,470,000 workers engaged in a variety of protests, from general strikes in Minneapolis, Toledo, and San Francisco to a national walkout of nearly 500,000 textile workers from South Carolina to Maine. These strikes reflected increased combativeness among unorganized workers, a growing influence of the left, and widespread antagonism toward the NRA and its pro-business codes.

When Democratic governors in twelve states used militia to break the textile workers' desperate strike, strikers became politicized and labor party sentiment grew. Though the Democrats swept the 1934 congressional elections, voters still expressed considerable interest in alternatives to the left of the New Deal. Roosevelt and the Democrats were clearly noticing the growing importance of the labor vote. In Pennsylvania, for example, working-class voters rejected the Republicans in boss-ridden coal and steel towns and helped the Democrats win substantial victories.

The impressive labor vote for liberal Democrats and for more radical candidates convinced Communist party leaders that the traditional party system might be breaking up and that the time was ripe for a farmer-labor party. This change of line conformed to the new "united front from below," in which the CP formed coalitions with Socialists and progressives who would aid in the world struggle against war and fascism. By mid-1935 the Popular Front had been adopted as world Communist policy; the CP in the United States agitated openly for a labor party within the AFL unions, which they had recently rejoined after abandoning their own Trade Union Unity League. The Socialists, who gave brief support to such a party, found themselves working with the Communists for the first time.

The New Deal was still unpopular in labor circles early in 1935 because of FDR's refusal to support Senator Robert Wagner's workers' rights bill. Distrust lingered even after the president changed his mind and signed the Wagner Act in May. At the AFL convention in October, Francis Gorman of the United Textile Workers led an unsuccessful fight for a labor party, with the support of Socialists, Communists, and industrial unionists.

Gorman, who had played key organizing roles in the southern textile strikes, reminded the delegates that Democratic governors used troops against the 1934 strikers. He also declared that the textile workers' standard of living had actually decreased under the NRA. "We looked with what now seems to us to be naive faith to the proponents of a 'New Deal'—believing, I guess, that it meant a New Deal for labor as well as industry," Gorman told the convention. "We have been sorely disappointed."

FDR HARNESSES THE LABOR VOTE

FDR's popularity increased in 1935. He was relieved of the NRA albatross in May, when it was declared unconstitutional. His support for the Wagner Act, social security, and other progressive measures of the "second New Deal" solidified his support among organized labor.

Political independents continued to win support in 1936, but efforts to form a national labor party in 1934 and 1936 failed, partly because of the reticence of the Socialists and the Communists' shifting commitment to the idea. Both left parties favored a farmer-labor formation, but they also had their own partisan interests to protect. When the United Mine Workers, the key force behind the CIO, endorsed FDR for a second term early in 1936, Norman Thomas and other farmer-laborites were discouraged.

John L. Lewis, who headed the UMW and the CIO, believed the new industrial unions needed the support, or at least the neutrality, of the president and Democratic officeholders. Lewis had fought bitterly with leftists and labor party supporters in the 1920s and he retained some of the old AFL reservations about entering politics. He also reflected an old syndicalist tradition in the American labor movement that emphasized union-building and placed little faith in partisan campaigning.

In the summer of 1936 Lewis formed Labor's Non-Partisan League (LNPL) to build labor support for Roosevelt's reelection. The LNPL also created the American Labor party in New York to win support for FDR, without having to ask workers, especially Socialists, to vote for the conservative Tammany Hall Democrats running for other offices. The LNPL did not, however, encourage the formation of labor parties in other states. In fact, in Massachusetts its leaders helped head off a fairly strong movement for a state farmer-labor party, and many suspected that the LNPL was, as Norman Thomas charged, no more than "a committee for Roosevelt" and a "tail on the Democratic kite."

 Party building in the 1930s showed that radical politics developed first at the local level, where it grew out of specific industrial and community struggles. Without this groundwork, neither the Communists, Socialists, nor farmer-laborites made significant gains.

In any case, the LNPL raised thousands of dollars and mobilized voters for FDR's reelection campaign. The president and New Deal Democrats swept the 1936 election, and farmer-labor parties made poor showings. The Socialists, who enjoyed some resurgence at the polls, were now discouraged about the chances for a farmer-labor party. But the Communist party believed that results of the 1936 election showed a sharpening of class lines in American politics. Its leaders stated that the time was now ripe for a multi-class third party in which the CP could participate without losing its identity. The CIO's expulsion from the AFL in 1936 and its victories in rubber, auto, steel, meatpacking, electrical manufacturing, and other industries seemed to provide the social base for a new party, the kind of base once afforded to the old Socialist party by the first industrial unions of miners, brewers, and clothing workers.

This prognosis proved incorrect for several reasons. First, the Socialists and Communists, who had supported farmer-labor party activity, contributed little after the 1936 election. The Socialist party was rent by faction fights and hurt by the loss of New York needle trade unionists to the ALP. The Communist party adopted a much weaker stance toward a farmer-labor party in 1937; its leaders were more anxious to gain a foothold in the CIO to advance the Popular Front against fascism than they were in building a socialist electoral alternative. Second, the CIO developed *after* the initial period of farmer-labor activity, and later third-party efforts had to buck the strong CIO-Democratic alliance.

Finally the Democrats made the most of the situation. Without making great concessions to organized labor, they won the support of CIO officials on the basis of FDR's belated support for the Wagner Act and the sore need for friendly or neutral office holders in strike situations. For example, in the great Flint sit-down strike of 1937 that allowed the UAW to win recognition at General Motors, FDR and Michigan's New Deal Governor Frank Murphy refused GM's call for troops to evict the strikers. Had either man ordered troops to evict the sit-downers, political history might have taken a different turn. Labor party sentiment, already on the rise in the UAW, might have been hard to resist. Instead, UAW leaders, preoccupied with building their union, joined other CIO officials in developing a working relationship with professional politicians in the Democratic party.

In 1937 the New Deal encountered further problems as unemployment shot back up, the conservatives gained in Congress, and the Roosevelt administration began to cut back relief jobs and to reduce its commitment to progressive social legislation. But by this time the CIO was already firmly wedded to the Democratic party. When CIO President John L. Lewis threatened to resign if FDR was nominated for a third term, he was forced to keep his word. Not only had Roosevelt won the support of Lewis's fellow CIO leaders; he had also gained the loyalty of millions of CIO rank and filers, despite the limitations of the New Deal. Southern reactionaries and other conservatives gained strength in the Democratic party, but most union workers loyally voted for FDR's fellow Democrats—except in New York and Minnesota, where viable labor parties allowed workers to split their tickets.

What did organized labor and the working class generally gain by giving such massive support to Roosevelt and the Democrats? One argument is that labor support in 1936 helped push the New Deal further to the left. In fact, most of the progressive legislation of the New Deal, notably the Wagner Act and direct work relief, came before the CIO entered politics. These reforms were more the product of mass unrest and direct action in militant strikes and demonstrations than of electoral activity.

Another view is that after 1936 the Democratic party became a surrogate labor party. After the CIO gave organized support to the Democrats, it gained more influence in the Roosevelt administration; but in fact few union members actually took positions in Washington, and when several (including Sidney Hillman) did enter the government during the war mobilization, they played second fiddle to businessmen and bureaucrats.

Important political changes did occur at the state and local levels during the 1930s. The victory of pro-CIO candidates in scores of Republican-controlled industrial cities was an important development. In some cases these candidates were workers themselves, but most were Democratic politicians who promised to represent workers. A stronger farmer-labor party movement during the 1930s, when the CIO was consolidating its strength, might have put far more working people in public office.

As it was, labor reformers attempted to represent workers within the New Deal wing of the Democratic party or the left wing of the Republican party. Some radical pro-labor politicians, such as Vito Marcantonio of New York, faithfully represented socially conscious unionism within the Democratic party. But by the late 1930s most New Deal politicians could take the labor vote for granted. FDR's popularity, the emphasis on lobbying Congress legislation, and the need for support from local Democratic officeholders made it difficult for unionized workers to choose political independence.

Still, the labor movement could have used its newly acquired political power more effectively. A unified left might have created a viable farmer-labor party, although such an effort would have required the Communists and Socialists to put aside their own partisan ambitions. Alternatively, the labor movement might have supported FDR without allowing itself to be thoroughly incorporated into the party, which still represented bankers, industrialists, small businessmen, and southern planters as well as workers. If the LNPL had encouraged and supported the formation of groups similar to the American Labor party in New York, there would have been a left alternative to the conservative and opportunistic Democratic politicians. Instead, as the Democratic party moved to the right and actually took anti-labor positions, unions lacked any independent electoral or organizational base from which to challenge the party from the inside or the outside.

IF NEGRO MEN
CAN CARRY GUNS FOR
UNCLE SAM
SURELY
THEY CAN DRIVE MILK
WAGONS FOR
BOWMAN DAIRY

Despite the gains blacks made during and after World War II, prejudice remained an important factor in employment. From Schnapper, *American Labor.*

Blacks and the CIO

Richard Thomas

From its inception the American labor movement has been dogged by the persistent problem of racism within its ranks. Yet the movement has also scored impressive victories over class and racial oppression, because of the persistent challenge of black trade unionists. By insisting on the needs of all segments of the working class, black or white, employed or unemployed, the black challenge has been a catalyst for social justice within the labor movement.

This black challenge goes back to 1869, when the Colored National Labor Union convened to protest exclusion from the mainstream of the white trade union movement. Later on, gallant struggles for racial equality were waged in the Noble Order of the Knights of Labor (which was dubbed by some as "the black International") and the Industrial Workers of the World.

Such struggles made little headway in the American Federation of Labor under the reign of Samuel Gompers. On the other hand, the Congress of Industrial Organizations had to be sensitive to racial realities in the mass-production industries of steel, rubber, auto, mining and meatpacking, where there were large concentrations of black workers. It was at this point that the black challenge to labor had its greatest impact.

Before the CIO recruitment drive among black industrial workers, the most direct challenge to labor was strikebreaking. Contrary to many popular beliefs, before the CIO came on the labor scene, strikebreaking had become a conscious aspect of intraclass struggles against the white workers' racial dominance in the workplace. The CIO was able to divert this aspect of the black challenge to labor into a temporary class challenge to capitalists.

From the very beginning the CIO promised black workers a fair shake. During the 1936–37 organizing drives in steel and autos, the CIO organized on an integrated basis. In 1939 the Georgia Ku Klux Klan "declared war" on the textile workers' organizing committee because of its interracial program. Such actions prompted the NAACP to comment, "It has often been said that you can tell a man by the kind of enemies he makes. If this is true of organizations also, then the CIO is certainly an unparalleled blessing in our land." The CIO went on to earn more praise from black leaders and workers when it assigned leadership positions to black workers.

Some black leaders remained skeptical because of their past experiences with the AFL. Lester Grange, speaking for the National Urban League, cautioned black workers against "jubilantly rushing toward what they assume to be a new day for labor and a new organization to take the place of the AFL." But it was not long before the CIO won the endorsement of the National Negro Congress. The NNC was founded in 1936 (just a few months after the founding of the CIO) by more than 250 influential blacks, who called for a National Negro Congress made up of all black organizations "from old-line Republican to Communist" to address the urgent problems of black people. Organizing black industrial workers was considered to be one of the most pressing of these problems.

At the first session of the NNC held in Chicago, A. Philip Randolph told the delegates representing 585 organizations that their special mission was to "draw Negro workers into labor organizations and break down the color bar in the trade unions that now have it."

The pro-labor orientation of the NNC was crucial at a time when the CIO needed all the help it could get. The NNC not only endorsed the CIO but also, because of its strong Communist elements, provided the new industrial union with its most radical support.

As the CIO met the black challenge by fighting against the racism of both capitalists and workers, it became known among the black community as its best ally. During the Ford strike of 1941 many conservative local black leaders took Henry Ford's side against the UAW-CIO. But after Ford went down to defeat and the UAW-CIO sided with black workers against white workers' attempts to prevent them from obtaining jobs in defense industries, the attitudes of these local black leaders changed drastically. By 1945 the black community, as one labor scholar has pointed out, "looked upon the CIO and the idea of labor solidarity as the black man's greatest hope for social and economic progress in the postwar period."

The honeymoon between black workers and the CIO soon ended, however. The persistent economic and social problems of black workers necessarily gave rise to new and more urgent challenges, many of which could not be effectively met by the CIO alone. The AFL was still very powerful and unrelenting in its racism. During their 1946 convention AFL members voted down resolutions to end segregated auxiliary locals. Meanwhile, the CIO was slowly losing its fighting spirit as it drifted into an "unholy alliance" with the AFL to discredit Communist-led unions.

Several years before their formal merger into the AFL-CIO, these two labor organizations competed with each other in driving out of the labor movement many of the very radicals who had worked hardest for black people. In fact, during World War II left-wing unions did more than other unions in promoting racial equality. Such unions as the United Packing House Workers, the International Fur and Leather Workers Union, the Marine Cooks and Stewards, among others, laid the foundation for interracial labor solidarity. When the radical elements in these unions were purged, black workers were forced to struggle almost alone against persistent racism in the labor movement.

The first significant postwar challenge occurred in 1950 in the form of the National Negro Labor Conference. It arose in a period of great hardship for black workers. Most of the economic advances made by black industrial workers occurred between 1942 and 1945 and were largely lost during the postwar reconversion of war industries into peacetime production. Reconversion fell most heavily on black industrial workers because of their greater concentration in unskilled war production jobs with the least possibility of reconversion to civilian production. In 1946 the Fair Employment Practices Commission's final report revealed that black workers were experiencing more unemployment than white workers in six of the seven war centers studied. The dire economic plight of black industrial workers was worsened by the government's failure to push for a strong permanent FEPC, without which black workers could not hope for much government protection.

As unemployment began steadily rising, many black workers began a descent into a permanent depression. On the heels of this job loss came a technological revolution that ate away at the heart of black employment—the unskilled and semi-skilled jobs. As northern black workers were struggling just to hold onto wartime gains, they were joined by tens of thousands of displaced southern black agricultural workers who were gradually being pushed northward by the impact of agricultural technology on the southern plantation economy. To compound hard times, organized labor in many ways was becoming part of the problem again, rather than part of the solution.

More than any other single segment of the American working class, black workers stood alone at this hour. Black middle-class organizations like the NAACP and the Urban League had no solutions to the problems of black workers. The promising National Negro Congress had lasted less than ten years, while the March on Washington Movement died during the postwar period.

But what about the labor movement and the promises of the CIO? Many white labor leaders believed they had met the major challenge of black workers by bringing them into the CIO on a nonracial basis and fighting for the rights of black workers to obtain jobs in the defense industries. These leaders failed to understand that the black working class had historically fought both a class and race struggle, and that to the black community the race struggle was much more compelling because it was being waged against both white capital and labor. The challenge facing leftists in the labor movement was to support black workers in both of these struggles. Unfortunately, even the most progressive segments failed to meet this challenge.

This challenge was voiced repeatedly at the National Labor Conference for Negro Rights held in Chicago in June 1950 (which led to the formation of the National Negro Labor Council a year later). The Communist party was among those initiating the NNLC and gave it active support throughout its existence. Black delegates from the AFL reported that the Federation was still discriminating against black workers. CIO black delegates accused it of retreating from its earlier position on the rights of black workers. All the delegates agreed that black workers were being discriminated against in apprenticeship training programs and that they were being barred from advancing into skilled and semi-skilled jobs by racist collective bargaining agreements.

Deciding the black workers had to take the lead in their own struggle, the Conference established a continuation committee composed of veteran black labor leaders. William R. Hood, recording secretary of Local 600, UAW-CIO, was made president of the committee; Cleveland Robinson, vice-president of the Distributive, Processing, and Office Workers Union (District 65), was made vice-president; and Coleman Young of the Amalgamated Clothing Workers staff, and by then a veteran labor leader in Detroit as well as former director of organization of the Wayne County CIO Council, was made executive secretary of the committee.

In less than a year this committee set up twenty-three Negro Labor Councils in major industrial cities, and these local NLCs immediately began combatting racial discrimination on all fronts. The NLC of Greater New York sprang into action a week after the natonal conference by calling a "Job Action Conference," which was attended by 250 trade unionists. They reported on problems in the building trades, printing, railroads, utilities, and other industries. The conference resulted in 250 jobs and a commitment from the public relations manager of Safeway stores promising that each qualified applicant would be given an equal opportunity for employment.

The NLC in Chicago began a drive against racial discrimination in the Woolworth and Scott stores, where blacks could shop but not work. The manager of Woolworth swore that he would not hire black saleswomen "until hell freezes over." But when the NLC set up picket lines around the stores, causing business to fall off by 85 percent, the stores gave up and hired black women. On the West Coast the NLC helped the Urban League in California's East Bay win a victory over the Key System Transit Lines, a local transport monopoly that had refused to hire black workers. The NLCs were equally effective in the South. The NLC led a successful struggle to force the Louisville Board of Education to prepare black workers for jobs that were to be opened by General Electric.

In 1951, during the NNLC's first campaign to have a "model FEPC clause" incorporated into every union contract, only the United Electrical and Radio Machine Workers Union (UE) did so. This union not only adopted the model clause as its official union policy but also set up a fair practices committee to take the lead in a "nationwide drive for the full rights of its black and women members." While left-wing trade unions, such as the Marine Cooks and Stewards and the International Longshoremen's and Warehousemen's Unions, offered their wholehearted support of the NLCs, other unions such as the UAW engaged in "red-baiting."

In Detroit one of the most successful NLCs, under the leadership of William R. Hood of Local 600, was a constant worry to the UAW leadership. The NLC and Walter Reuther did not see eye to eye on the former's petition drive for a local FEPC ordinance. Reuther, along with seven other international officers, ordered all auto workers who had signed the petition to withdraw their names, calling the people behind the drive "irresponsible" and "Communist-inspired" because they had not consulted with the UAW-CIO.

But the conflict between black workers in the Detroit NLC and the UAW leadership went deeper than the clash over the FEPC drive. For several years black workers had been challenging the UAW's all-white male leadership to push more vigorously for the upgrading of black workers as well as the inclusion of blacks on the UAW's major policy making body, the International Executive Board. The UAW's failure to meet this challenge led black workers to continue their own independent struggles against the racism of both capitalists and labor.

Led by the Detroit NLC, black NLCs around the nation held a conference in October 1951 to set up a National Negro Labor Council (NNLC). Several white labor leaders of the AFL and the CIO accused the convention of "dual unionism." Organizers denied the charge and defined the NNLC's objective as building a new organization to encourage black workers to join unions and encourage unions to organize black workers. The delegates also informed their white trade union critics that "that day has ended when white trade union leaders or white leaders in any organization may presume to tell Negroes on what basis they shall come together to fight for their rights.... We ask your cooperation— but we do not ask your permission!"

The convention adopted two major tasks for itself: to defeat racial discrimination in industry, and to eliminate racism in the trade union movement and use it as a base from which trade unions and progressive white allies could struggle for the economic liberation of blacks. No sooner had the goals been stated than the newly formed organization was attacked by white CIO leaders, led by James B. Carey, as a tool of the Soviet Union. Such attacks masked the fears and unwillingness of many white labor leaders adequately to assess independent black working-class organizations. The red-baiting and "dual unionism" accusations helped pave the way for the House Committee on

Un-American Activities (HUAC) to harass the NNLC. Such harassment, along with other adverse pressures, forced the demise
of the NNLC in 1956.

Racism within the ranks of labor remained an issue, particularly after the merger of the AFL-CIO in 1955. Many black trade
unionists saw the merger as a signal of organized labor's declining
interest and commitment to the struggle against racism. Notwithstanding the vague promises of equality put into the new
organization's constitution, black workers were well aware of the
lack of enforcement that rendered such promises meaningless.
The AFL-CIO constitution provided sanctions against affiliates
dominated by "Communists" while providing little or no sanction
against affiliates dominated by racists. It was clear that such a
challenge—namely, to provide protection for nonwhite workers
against union racism—was not to be taken seriously. No wonder,
then, that five years later, in 1960, the NAACP's labor secretary, Herbert Hill, revealed that many AFL-CIO affiliates were
yet restricting black workers to segregated locals, that black auto
and steel workers were yet confined to unskilled jobs, and
that several southern affiliates were working with White Citizens' Councils.

By 1960 American labor still had a long way to go in meeting
the black challenge. While prominent white labor leaders would
march alongside blacks in the great civil rights demonstrations in
Detroit, Washington, and Selma and would endorse the principle
of equality in theory, they would fail to mount a strong and
persistent struggle against racism within their own ranks. This
failure to mount such a struggle left a vacuum that would only be
filled by independent black labor organizations.

Gathering to protest Taft-Hartley at the 1948 AFL convention. Photo courtesy of
George Meany Memorial Archives.

Labor and the Cold War

George Lipsitz

American labor responded to the end of World War II with one of the largest strike waves in the nation's history. More than a release of frustration, the widespread demonstrations and wildcat strikes expressed an unwillingness of workers to return to Depression era economics and a demand for direct means to control their own destiny. Direct action, a strategy for pressuring an unresponsive system, became also an end in itself. Alone, that action could not transcend the political limitations on labor militancy (given the host of anti-labor bills pushed through Congress) or the establishment of a bureaucratic labor peace between big business and top union leadership. Yet mass activism placed limits upon the political process and laid down essential hints for the future of American radicalism.

THE 1945–46 STRIKE WAVE

Shortly before the end of the war, workers in a Detroit auto plant walked off their jobs over an apparently trivial dispute about lunchroom recreation. Less than a year later striking steelworkers in Fairfield, Alabama, filled the street in front of the mill and "demonstrated" by holding a jitterbug dance. A citywide strike supported by teamsters in Oakland, California, late in 1946 so exasperated that union's international president that he condemned it as "a lot of damn foolishness with no rhyme, reason, or sense, more like a revolution than an industrial dispute." These strikes did contain fanciful and utopian elements indicative of a desire to enjoy life despite the hardships of work, but they also entailed quite serious attempts to combine immediate needs with long-range utopian goals.

Workers suffered serious reverses as soon as the war ended. Cutbacks in production ended the availability of overtime work and the accompanying bonus pay, and nearly one-quarter of all war workers temporarily lost their jobs as factories retooled for civilian production. Throughout the war businessmen and economists had warned that full employment could not continue once the conflict ended, and so these cutbacks seemed to foreshadow a drop in the high employment levels attained during the war. Strikes took place all over the country because of fear of postwar unemployment. The concerns of many were voiced by machinists in Stamford, Connecticut, who launched a strike under a banner reading "We will not go back to the old days."

Tax breaks made it easy for companies to endure strikes during the first year after the war's end, and union leaders were reluctant to call their members out on strike. But the rank and file forced the issue, insisting on striking to maintain wartime levels of employment and income. Unionists also viewed the strike as a means of building a postwar world with good working conditions, abundant consumer goods, and some political counterforce to the concentrated power of big business. They believed that collective mass action was the only way to shape the country on their terms.

During the winter of 1945–46 strikes shut down the steel, electrical, and auto industries. During the auto workers' strike at General Motors the union demanded that wage increases come out of profits and not be passed on to consumers in the form of higher prices. That kind of demand, which mobilized the power of workers for the public good, epitomized the radical spirit behind the postwar strikes. The settlement of that strike without the meeting of that demand established a long-standing pattern of consumers underwriting the wage gains of organized labor. Profits remain secure, while some workers gain at the expense of others.

The 1945–46 strike wave won some important wage gains for workers in labor unions, but it brought reverses as well. Prices increased by 16 percent after the strikes, and the strikers lost over $1 billion in wages. Union leaders such as the UAW's R. J. Thomas and Walter Reuther made important concessions to employers, giving them more freedom to discipline the workforce and control production. Yet the strikers did win important victories on the local level, establishing themselves as spokespersons for the common good. Communities rallied to their support with food kitchens and support committees. Despite the disruptions and inconveniences of the strikes, polls conducted for *Fortune* magazine indicated that workers gained and management lost favor with the public as the strikes continued. A series of general strikes that paralyzed production and mobilized public opinion in a number of cities in 1946 provide the best evidence of the extent and limits of working-class political power during that era.

THE GENERAL STRIKES OF 1946

More than 10,000 people streamed into Atlantic Square in Stamford, Connecticut, on the cold, clear morning of January 3, 1946, as part of the first American general strike in twelve years. Six weeks later roving picket lines closed down all business in Lancaster, Pennsylvania, for three days; more than 14,000 workers stayed away from their jobs. A similar demonstration erupted in Rochester, New York, in late May, when a general strike halted business and brought thousands of curious and jubilant citizens into the downtown district. In September the imprisonment of a labor leader on contempt of court charges brought thousands of workers into a general work stoppage that paralyzed Pittsburgh for weeks. More than 100,000 workers participated in a general strike in Oakland, California, in December, closing down businesses, stopping traffic, and administering vital city services on their own.

In their resort to mass direct action these strikes challenged the form of government and business collusion refined during World War II and even more fully administered in subsequent years.

Government raised capital for private industry, and agencies composed of representatives of business, labor, and government gained unprecedented power to oversee the economy in the name of uninterrupted production and high profits. Leaders of interest groups gained powerful positions in government by presuming to speak for their segment of society, but the individual worker, farmer, voter, or consumer felt an increasing sense of powerlessness. Frustrated by the workings of this system during the war, workers in the postwar era created their own instruments of direct democracy, bypassing "legitimate" but unresponsive channels in favor of mass demonstrations and disruptions. Every protest movement since that time has followed this example. A system based on stability is especially vulnerable to disruptive protest. Once the state tries to impose labor peace, working-class demands become challenges to state power. In a world of bureaucracy, direct action is the great equalizer.

The 1946 general strikes posed direct challenges to legitimate political authority and property rights. Workers in Stamford and Lancaster battled with police officers, while strikers in Rochester and Pittsburgh defied direct orders from city hall. Corporate spokesmen in Stamford accused the city government of condoning illegal violence, while lawyers for the struck company in Lancaster refused to negotiate in the midst of what they termed "bloodshed and riot." Rochester's city manager argued that the strikers threatened to destroy city government, and the city lawyer in Pittsburgh asked for an injunction against that strike because of its threat to "life, health, and property." Oakland's mayor lambasted the local strike as "an attempt to push aside the government created by all the people" and to "substitute the physical force of mobs for that of government." He was absolutely right; the amazing thing is that so many of Oakland's citizens supported that effort.

The participants in the 1946 general strikes had no expectation that a revolution would take place as a result of their efforts; they had no conscious intention of overthrowing the government. These strikes began as labor-management disputes confined to relatively small groups of workers, but in each case the public at large became involved in order to remedy injustice or to advance their concept of fair play. When local governments used police violence or companies refused to bargain in good faith, ordinary workers spontaneously walked off their jobs in support of others. Speaking not only for themselves but for their class, they demanded fair treatment for workers. They also represented aspirations for a higher standard of living and a more democratic society among the public at large. Once the strikes began and ordinary citizens became involved in directing traffic, distributing goods, and managing the affairs of their communities, they got a taste of a new kind of politics—and they liked it.

Critics decried the carnival-like atmosphere of the strikes, but that communal joy was a public issue. When people who had been distant suddenly found themselves confronting each other in serious decisionmaking, when thoroughfares suddenly became playgrounds, and when repressed aspirations for having some voice in community affairs suddenly became reality, a sense of exhilaration resulted. The strikes were fun, they were effective in winning their short range goals, and they gave millions of people a glimpse of the politics of direct democracy.

The general strikes of 1946 proved to be serious threats to the authority of business and government. They motivated those in power to fashion repressive measures designed to wrest political leadership away from the working class so that the powerful could go on reorganizing the postwar world on terms favorable to big business.

THE TAFT-HARTLEY ACT

The success of the 1946 strikes, big business's desire to control production and secure high profits, and anti-labor publicity in the news media all contributed to the pressure for repressive legislation, notably the Taft-Hartley Act. The original impetus for the bill came from small businessmen, whose labor costs were a large part of their expenses. Although government spending during the war mostly aided big business at the expense of small entrepreneurs, the latter's pro-business ideology and traditional hatred of unions made them blame their declining position on labor. Big businessmen naturally encouraged the small business attack on labor. Although they had more of their capital tied up in machinery and could afford to make some concessions to workers in return for uninterrupted production, big businessmen nonetheless wanted to keep labor costs as low as possible. They needed strong government regulation of the economy and high federal spending to keep their production at highly profitable wartime levels. They knew they could use small businessmen's fear of labor to get them to agree to government regulation of labor-management relations, while using labor's fear of the small business offensive to force unions to accept limits on their own power.

Taft-Hartley banned the tactics prominent in the 1946 general strikes including secondary boycotts, mass picketing, and sympathy strikes. It also made unions responsible for damage caused by wildcat strikes sanctioned by "unions or their agents," in an effort to force unions to assume a greater role in policing the rank and file. In addition, the bill allowed states to ban the union shop, required union leaders to sign non-Communist affidavits in order to win NLRB protection for their unions, and increased the power of the president to obtain injunctions against strikes.

The Republican victory in the 1946 congressional elections and a postwar electoral trend away from New Deal ideology contributed to the passage of Taft-Hartley, as did some highly publicized and unpopular strikes in the railroad and mining industries. President Truman vetoed the bill (Congress passed it over his objections) despite the fact that he had previously proposed every position in it at one time or another, and even after labor contributed to the return of a Democratic congressional majority in 1948 the act was not repealed. Labor leaders themselves generally found that they could live with Taft-Hartley. They genuinely opposed Section 14(B), allowing states to ban the union shop, but found that the prohibitions against wildcat strikes and the penalties against Communist union leaders enabled them to maintain undisputed control over their organizations.

THE COLD WAR

Prominent business leaders feared renewed depression once wartime production ended. Workers demanded full employment; small businessmen wanted lower government spending. Yet the economy's wartime health depended on that spending and its resulting high employment. The only way to maintain high levels of production and employment would be through a combination of overseas economic expansion and renewed military spending.

Hostilities between the United States and the Soviet Union provided the opportunity to realize both goals. Anticommunism made economic expansion overseas a matter of patriotic obligation, while equating opposition to that policy with disloyalty. It gave the government a means of stimulating production, raising taxes, increasing the military budget, and silencing opposition at home.

One potential source of opposition came from labor, and the Truman administration directed great energy toward neutralizing that threat. Secretary of State George Marshall addressed the 1947 CIO convention, urging labor to fulfill its proper role by supporting government policies overseas. One year later Supreme Court Justice William O. Douglas urged the same body to eliminate "extremists both Right and Left"—a none too subtle reference to Communists in the labor movement. If labor leaders wanted a role in government policymaking, they had to subdue Communists and all other compatriots opposed to Truman's foreign policy. In 1949 the CIO expelled a number of unions whose leaders refused to sign the non-Communist affidavits of Taft-Hartley and who opposed the Cold War. It is important to remember that this expulsion took place largely at the upper levels; there was little grass-roots pressure for purging Communists from unions. The call came from the top and was most successful on that level, although the purge did have its effects on the rank and file.

Communists found themselves politically vulnerable in the postwar period because of their leaders' record during the war. They had supported the no-strike pledge, zealously condemned wildcat strikers, and called for continued labor-management cooperation in the postwar world. Yet even without their poor record on wartime shop-floor activism, their miscalculations about the postwar world, and their awkward dependence on the foreign policy interests of the Soviet Union, Communists in labor would still have been tied to forms of organization that inevitably placed them in direct opposition to the strategies behind the postwar strike wave.

Communists in the labor movement assumed that unions and workers had identical interests, that union successes would build working-class power, and that leadership in unions translated into leadership of the working class. This analysis wedded them to the bureaucratic union structure. Despite extraordinary bravery displayed by individual Communists, despite excellent records against racial discrimination and sexism, most Communists in the labor movement remained out of touch with the emerging consciousness of direct action. On the local level, those Communists who had good reputations with the rank and file commanded enormous loyalty. Yet that popularity stemmed from their role in supporting grass-roots working-class activism, not from distinctly communist policies. The expulsion of Communists from the CIO opened new positions for anti-Communist labor leaders in the higher circles of power; it also lessened the likelihood of internal union rivalries, thus limiting democratic debate within unions, but it only incidentally attacked the interests of the rank and file.

NEW POLITICS AND OLD POLITICS

Struggles between Republicans and Democrats on the national level and fights between Communists and anti-Communists within unions revolved around the question of who would control increasingly bureaucratic institutions in government and organized labor. The working-class strategies of independence manifested in the general strikes of 1946 raised a radical vision of politics concerned with direct decisionmaking, not with control of key institutions. Those strikes were opposed to *bureaucracy itself;* they did not revolve around who *controlled* the bureaucracy. Opposed to state power, they did not seek a role in administering the state. Liberals and leftists within unions and the Democratic party promised workers that they would restrain anti-labor forces and advance labor's interests within the system. But for many in the rank and file, the problem was increasingly becoming the system itself.

This is not to say that the workers involved in the general strikes and mass demonstrations of the postwar era saw their own actions as revolutionary efforts to overthrow the state. Some did—but most simply responded to the needs of the moment. Their opposition to authority, to work, to hierarchical power drew upon deep currents of resistance embeddened in American working-class history. Yet throughout that history workers have known that their desires for autonomy are illegitimate by society's standards. Like stealing supplies at work or walking out over a grievance even when you know you're wrong, resistance with no legitimate justification persists because it challenges the legitimacy of the system of industrial capitalism. Such resistance is usually covert and short lived, because workers know it is illegitimate. The militant but brief resistance of the postwar general strikes expressed that sensibility. Workers could not translate their aspirations into legitimate programmatic alternative be- cause their real demands were so radical that they could not be satisfied or legitimated within the system. Electoral politics and trade union reform may have offered more equity within the system, but they could not challenge the system itself and therefore could not speak to underlying aspirations for independence. For those aspirations to be fulfilled, workers would need more than the respectability granted by the system. They would need to project a worldview in which their desires for freedom and community were legitimate and in which the imperatives of work, hierarchy, and exploitation were illegitimate.

CONCLUSION

After the Taft-Hartley Act, the Cold War, and the expulsion of Communists from the CIO, unions conceded much to big business and big government. The impulses behind the strategies of independence did not disappear; they simply lacked institutional focus. Attendance at meetings dropped after 1950 in most unions, but wildcat strikes persisted as an expression of shop-floor discontent. As capitalists passed the indirect costs of production onto consumers and taxpayers, traditionally working-class forms of opposition spread throughout society. The civil rights, student, antiwar, and women's movements of succeeding years all drew upon the tactics and aspirations manifest in the postwar general strikes.

 One of the most important facets of the 1946 strikes was the ability of workers to transform their own immediate demands into a strategy and philosophy capable of speaking for the community at large. In their belief in direct decisionmaking, their use of small-group and mass mobilization, and their perception that bureaucracy actually made the system more vulnerable to disruption, they led the way for subsequent movements for social change.

If class is to have meaning as more than a code word for one set of interests, it lies in the way one group can make its own interests synonymous with the emancipation of others. Working-class strategies of independence established that dynamic on a political level, while working-class culture fought a similar battle in other spheres. Music that began as the rhythm and blues and country music of some groups of workers flowered into the music of all America in the form of rock and roll. Working-class artists and engineers who pioneered car customizing and racing in the postwar years created styles that drew such popular allegiance that Detroit soon followed suit. The speech and dress of urban blacks and Chicanos manifested in the zoot suits and "hip" talk of the war and postwar years became the dress and speech of young people and then adults from all classes. Working-class culture was transformed when it became a mass marketed commodity, but it became that commodity because it carried a sense of creativity and celebration that proved therapeutic to other groups.

The mass activism of the postwar era forcefully opposed a return to depression levels of unemployment and short-circuited the emergence of an anti-labor campaign on the scale of the one that followed World War I. It pressured business and government into foreign and domestic policies that brought a revolution in consumer spending and that turned previous luxuries into commonplace possessions. Perhaps labor's greatest advances came in the grandiose if still unrealized longings for emancipation from exploitation and hierarchy that manifested themselves in the joyous general strikes, mass demonstrations, and new cultural forms of the era.

A woman on the picket line. Photo courtesy of Earl Dotter/American Labor Education Center.

Women Workers

Barbara Mayer Wertheimer

For the first time in history more than half of all American women work outside the home. For these women, inside or out of labor unions, a struggle is going on for space in what still is a man's world. This struggle was defined by A. Philip Randolph: "At the banquet table of nature there are no reserved seats. You get what you can take. To do that, you need power."

When women won the vote in 1920 neither economic nor political power was redistributed. The vote came, in a sense, during World War I, when women had moved into heavy industry and had taken over food production on the nation's farms. They had made a contribution that could not be denied. At the same time, women's role in the home continued to shift from domestic production to maintenance. Household appliances deskilled her work, reduced her status, and freed her for jobs in burgeoning offices, department stores, and services.

The need for income that brought women to the workplace then transformed them into special victims of the Great Depression. Government employment and recovery programs included few of the 3.5 million unemployed women. Many young women left home to avoid burdening their families; thousands slept in railroad and subway stations; many resorted to tenement homework as they sought any way at all to earn money.

The Congress of Industrial Organizations included women and minority workers for the first time on a large scale. Between 1933 and 1938 union membership rose from 3 to 8 million. Thousands of workers sat in, taking over factories to win union recognition. Women were part of that struggle in garment plants, Pennsylvania coal towns, five-and-dime stores in New York, drug stores in Detroit, pecan farms in Texas. Women earned their union spurs on an equal footing with men.

World War II turned out to be a watershed for workforce women. Women's employment rose from 14 million to 20.6 million at the height of the war. One and a half million black women held factory jobs, many of them for the first time. Married women made up a high proportion of the workforce, also for the first time. Following the war some women were laid off and left the workforce for homemaking, but most did not. Displaced from higher-paying war industry jobs, thousands took lower-paying jobs in offices, stores, restaurants, and household work. By 1950 almost as many women once again were in the workforce as at the height of the war. And the participation of women in the labor force continued to grow.

WHY DO WOMEN WORK?

Why do 52 percent of all adult women now work? Women work for the same reasons that men do: they support or help to support their families. More than three-fourths of all employed women either support themselves and their families or are married to men who earn less than $15,000 a year. Women are 75 percent of all Americans living in poverty and head 49 percent of all poor families. Where they do not head families, the sharp inflation of the 1970s has frequently made a second income essential.

Demographic factors also contribute. In 1920 women's life expectancy was forty-eight years; today it is seventy-six years or more. Thus a woman can expect at least twenty-five years of work-life after her last child is born. In addition, workers seek, often at great personal sacrifice, to educate their children, and the rising cost of education puts additional pressure on women. Finally, as the American workforce shifted from blue collar to white, millions of jobs opened up in traditional fields of women's work: health care, education, sales, restaurant and food service, recreation, and office work. But increased job opportunities have not brought an increase in women's earnings, which average 59 cents for every dollar that a man earns. The wage gap exists even where women work in the same occupation, because they tend still to hold the least skilled, lowest-paying jobs in every category.

The civil rights movement of the 1950s and 1960s turned the nation's attention to social inequities. Heroic group pressure finally forced civil rights legislation, including the Equal Pay Act and Title VII of the Civil Rights Act, to deal with inequities in employment and pay. For the first time the law included a ban on employment discrimination based on sex.

In the midst of the tumultuous 1960s the women's movement was reborn. When the National Organization for Women was founded in 1966 it was primarily a middle-class organization. It had little appeal to working-class women, who shied away from the NOW marches and demonstrations. But both the women's movement and working women have changed so that today union and other working women join with NOW in political and legislative efforts for the Equal Rights Amendment and to pass laws to obtain a federally funded child care program and paid maternity leave, equal pay for equal work, and flexible hours and equitable social security.

WOMEN IN THE LABOR MOVEMENT

Within the last decade the number of women in labor unions or employee associations increased from 5.4 million to 6.9 million. It is no surprise that the fastest-growing unions are in occupations with a heavy preponderance of women workers: health care, government employment, and teaching. Still, in spite of the increase in the number of women in unions, only 15 percent of all women workers are organized. Nor has this rise in membership kept up with the number of women coming into the labor market.

Women join unions, as men do, because the union is the only

institution through which workers can challenge authority on a systematic, day-to-day basis. The alternative is to be virtually powerless at the workplace. While women on the average earn only 59 cents for every dollar men earn, union women earn 73 cents for every dollar union men earn. The dollar value of unions to women has been calculated to average $2,000 a year.

Few women outside unions have pension plans where they work, and medical coverage, maternity and sick leave, and other fringe benefits such as paid vacations and holidays often are better under a union agreement. Grievance procedure, the right to take up complaints including those centering on sexual harassment and race and sex discrimination, are workplace rights under most contracts. Many unions offer services such as counseling, legal aid, summer camps for children, negotiated tuition refund programs, and credit unions that provide a support system particularly utilized by female heads of families. Union conferences, education programs, and committees where women participate provide not only a social but also a creative outlet for abilities often stifled in the routine jobs that many women hold. It is not hard to understand, then, why women rank as the most loyal union members; for many the union is a home away from home.

WOMEN IN UNION LEADERSHIP

The 1970s was a decade of mobilization, a time of support groups, women's caucuses, and workplace organizing committees. Several international unions set up women's departments. Thanks in part to the women's movement, workforce women read about themselves in the press and saw more sensible portrayals of women on television and in films.

In the early 1970s the country's attention was riveted on a major and lengthy strike of Mexican-American workers in the Southwest, most of them women, against Farah, a clothing manufacturer. A nationwide boycott in support of these strikers became an important element in their ultimate victory and united unionists, students, church and women's groups, minority group organizations, and many political leaders in "La Causa."

In the 1970s, too, films documenting the lives of working-class women began to win awards: *Harlan County, With Babies and Banners, Norma Rae.* Lawsuits initiated by women, minorities, and unions on behalf of both turned into victories in the equal employment field, opening nontraditional and managerial positions to women and bringing back-pay awards and out-of-court settlements requiring company affirmative action programs. Unions, now responsible (under Title VII) along with management for acts of discrimination, began to train stewards to take up grievances on sex and race discrimination and to negotiate contracts that clearly spelled out a nondiscrimination policy.

But union leadership remains largely a white male bastion. There are many reasons for this. First, there are social barriers such as family responsibilities, fear of traveling at night, inability to find child care, husbands who don't want wives to participate. Second are job-related barriers, for example, the fact that active union women find supervisors harder on them than on active union men. And third, there is the lack of union leadership training for women.

Recently power has come to union women in a form uniquely their own, an organization that in six short years has had an impact far in excess of its small numbers and whose president, Joyce D. Miller, has become the first woman to sit on the executive council of the AFL-CIO. The Coalition of Labor Union Women (CLUW) was founded in 1974 by women who felt that for too long they had been functioning purely in support roles in their unions and that the time had come to win some power in the labor movement.

CLUW united women from independent unions, AFL-CIO unions, and employee associations to work across all jurisdictional lines for four major goals: affirmative action in the workplace and in the union; support for organizing the unorganized, particularly women; achieving the legislative and political goals of women workers, including getting more women elected to political office at all levels; and increasing the participation of women in their unions and associations.

Through a growing number of chapters around the country, rank-and-file union women have established a structure that provides them with the chance to learn firsthand how union politics work. They obtain practice in running for office, public speaking, organizing and chairing committees, leading demonstrations, and taking the responsibility for building CLUW chapters. It is therefore no surprise that CLUW women have been moving into local leadership and staff jobs.

As women take on new responsibilities and compete against men for union office, their power is recognized. Union leaders now find it essential to include women at conferences, state conventions, and on international union executive boards. When women are not included it is now an embarrassment to the leadership. Union women are outspoken, assertive, knowledgeable of their rights. They will be denied no longer.

BLACK AND WHITE TOGETHER

A well-known union song has a verse that begins, "Black and white together, we shall not be moved." In recent years black and white women have moved closer together. The wage gap between white women and black women has almost disappeared, but both groups have experienced a widening gap between their average earnings and those of men. Increasing numbers of minority women have moved into office and other white-collar jobs. In 1965, 60 percent of black women were in the same occupational categories as white women; in 1977, 79 percent were. A higher percentage of black women than white now belong to labor unions and employee associations: 24 percent of black women workers compared to 15 percent of white women.

Black women who have achieved positions of influence and high visibility increasingly report that, while on their way up, they experienced more discrimination because of sex than because of race. For example, in 1970 Congresswoman Shirley

Chisholm (D-N.Y.) said, "When I decided to run for Congress I knew I would encounter both anti-black and anti-female sentiment. What surprised me was the much greater virulence of sex discrimination."

SEXUAL HARASSMENT ON THE JOB

Sexual harassment on the job always has been a problem for women workers, whether slaves or free, in the home or in the factory or office. Only recently has it come into the open, freeing women to talk about harassment without shame and without feeling responsible for the harassment they endure. Wherever women workers gather this subject is discussed. It is particularly hard for women moving into nontraditional jobs in skilled trades or in work such as coalmining, truckdriving, or as dock laborers.

Several national unions have urged their locals to determine the extent of the problem, to discuss the issue at union functions, and to indicate official union disapproval of sexual harassment in any form. Stewards are encouraged to take up grievances on this issue. Model contract clauses banning harassment and joint labor-management committees to deal with the problem are two other approaches. Women's committees are forming to provide support to women grieving this issue and to sponsor education programs on the law and inform women on how to compile evidence for taking up sexual harassment grievances.

For other unions, however, having women members is fairly new, and representing women in nontraditional jobs is even newer. Many of their women members are people of great courage, breaking ground for others who will come after. Support through groups such as CLUW or the growing networks of women in skilled trades and crafts is essential.

WHITE-COLLAR WORKERS

At a time when factories are moving out of the country and assembly lines are being automated, office work and service jobs are the predicted growth sectors of the economy. In New York City, for example, a net job loss is projected over the coming decade, but office jobs will increase by 8 percent.

If the labor movement is to grow, it must look to the organization of the millions of workers in offices and the service occupations who are now unorganized. Several organized groups of women office workers now exist. One of these, Nine to Five, was launched in 1973. Within two years it had enough strength to seek affiliation with the Service Employees International Union (SEIU) and to establish Local 925, which has won several union elections and contracts in the Boston area. The SEIU finances the local's organizing staff, but the local conducts its own activities without interference, calling on SEIU services as needed—for example, its legal and research departments or pension and medical plan experts.

Direct action organizing, the method used by the Coalition of Labor Union Women as well as by the growing number of women office-worker groups, seems the most effective way to involve members in learning by doing. The leaders of these organizations have an unerring eye for publicity and use the media and the press with a sharply honed effectiveness. For example, with the help of Jane Fonda, who has made their cause her own, the National Association of Office Workers has taken over the traditional National Secretaries' Day. The slogan "Raises, not Roses," plus widely publicized demonstrations and rallies, focus on the timeworn custom of flowers or candy from the boss, thus underscoring the dignity that office workers seek.

This association speaks for the growing concern over automation, which it estimates will involve at least 1.5 million offices in the decade ahead. Robots and computers functioning on their own don't complain, don't organize, never need coffee breaks or maternity leaves, and never strike. Highly sophisticated methods of transmitting and storing information, using microprocessors and computer chips, will eliminate the need for many personal secretaries.

Resistance to office automation may be just the issue around which women office workers and the labor movement can organize the country's clerical and secretarial workforce. The labor movement takes this challenge seriously: in January 1980 the Industrial Union Department of the AFL-CIO co-sponsored, with CLUW, a national organizing conference to discuss strategies. If the labor movement commits funds and staff—women organizers especially—to the task, women workers may be the major thrust in unionization in the next few years.

In 1980, just when organizing the unorganized had become the mission of the Coalition of Labor Union Women, a Republican administration pledged to extending "right to work" laws entered office. The Republican platform repudiates the Equal Rights Amendment and supports a youth minimum wage, which directly affects minorities and women in low-paying jobs. In the coming years there may be a halt in enforcement of affirmative action and Title VII actions. Under the guise of protecting the family, we may see efforts to make women feel increasingly guilty if they work. Budget slashing means cuts in social services, directly affecting women with families who are the primary users of many of these services.

For workforce women, then, a new look at alliances is imperative. With the labor movement reexamining its political action, the opportunity for women's full participation has never been better. CLUW is growing and so is its role in readying women for leadership. The expanding organization of white-collar workers, the National Association of Office Workers, is raising women's awareness of the need for collective action. The next few years may bring new alliances between women inside and those outside the labor movement, targeting their common cause.

The answer to the 1980s swing to the right may lie in this growing understanding on the part of working women of their potential power. With new coalitions, women can come together to make use of that power at last. As Frederick Douglass said back in 1857, "Power concedes nothing without demand; it never did and it never will." Perhaps today the decade of demand is at hand.

Martin Luther King, Jr. (top center, in profile) led many of the protests of the 1950s and '60s and rallied the support of labor leaders, such as Walter Reuther, to the civil rights cause. Photo courtesy of George Meany Memorial Archives.

Black Insurgency

Manning Marable

Over fifteen years have passed since the major upheavals of black
workers, youth, and students in the black power and civil rights
movements. Black political militancy left the streets and lunch
counters, descending into factories and shops across the country.
Both black nationalism and integration drew heavily upon
worker unrest at the point of production, creating new and
dynamic organizations: the League of Revolutionary Black
Workers in Detroit; the Black Panther Caucus at the Fremont,
California, General Motors plant; and the United Black Brotherhood in Mahwah, New Jersey. In the Deep South, civil rights
activists from the Southern Christian Leadership Conference
helped to organize sanitation workers' strikes in St. Petersburg,
Atlanta, and Memphis. Ralph D. Abernathy, Hosea Williams,
Coretta Scott King, and A. Philip Randolph supported the
vigorous unionization efforts of the American Federation of
State, County and Municipal Employees. Abernathy, Williams,
and Andrew Young were arrested for nonviolently blocking the
path of garbage trucks in Atlanta, and the first two were again
arrested in Charleston, South Carolina, for supporting Local
1199 in its attempts to unionize hospital employees. By September 1972 hundreds of black trade unionists, led by AFSCME
Secretary-Treasurer William Lucy and Cleveland Robinson,
president of the Distributive Workers of America, created the
Coalition of Black Trade Unionists in Chicago. At its second
annual convention, held in Washington on May 25–27, 1973,

125

1,141 black delegates representing thirty-three unions were in attendance; 35–40 percent were black women.

It cannot be overemphasized that the civil rights and black power movements were fundamentally working-class and poor people's movements. From the very beginning, progressive unions were involved in the desegregation campaigns. The United Auto Workers, United Packinghouse Workers (District 65, Local 1199 in New York City), and the Brotherhood of Sleeping Car Porters all contributed funds to Martin Luther King Jr.'s Montgomery bus boycott of 1955–56. In rural areas of the Black Belt, small independent black farmers risked their families' safety by opening their homes to freedom riders and field secretaries of the Student Nonviolent Coordinating Committee. Black farmworkers, sharecroppers, service workers, and semi-skilled operatives were the great majority of those foot soldiers who challenged white hegemony at Selma's Pettus Bridge and in the streets of Birmingham.

Civil rights activists soon recognized the need to develop an employment strategy for blacks. In November 1963 a number of labor unions financed a conference at Howard University that brought together democratic socialists, trade union organizers, and radical civil rights activists. Civil rights workers, black and white, recognized by late 1964 that demands for desegregating the South's society lacked economic direction. In 1965 Jessie Morris, SNCC's field secretary in Mississippi, helped establish the Poor People's Corporation. Serving as its executive secretary, Morris funneled financial aid to various labor projects initiated by poor black workers. That same year the Mississippi Freedom Labor Union was created by two Council of Federated Organizations staff members. The historian Clay Carson relates that "within a few months, the MFLU attracted over a thousand members in several counties through its demands for a $1.25 an hour minimum wage, free medical care, social security, accident insurance, and equality for blacks in wages, employment opportunities, and working conditions." MFLU relied upon SNCC fund-raising resources and "by that fall had developed its own sources of financial support."

As "We Shall Overcome" gave ground to "Black Power" in the mid-1960s, a wave of nationalist activism seized the new generation of black urban workers and students. Militant black construction unions were formed, such as Trade Union Local 124 in Detroit and United Community Construction Workers of Boston. Black steelworkers at Sparrows Point, Maryland, formed the Shipyard Workers for Job Equality, pressuring Bethlehem Steel to halt its policies of hiring and promoting discrimination against blacks. Most protest actions displayed the recognition that racism in the plants also undercut the economic status of white workers. For example, when the United Black Brothers struck at Mahwah's auto plant in April 1969, they urged white workers to "stay out and support us in this fight."

By the 1980s much of the political terrain had shifted to the right. White blue-collar workers voted strongly for Ronald Reagan. The League of Revolutionary Black Workers, the Black Panther Labor caucuses, and other revolutionary nationalist organizations within the black working class no longer existed. A. Philip Randolph had participated in the senatorial campaign for the neoconservative Daniel Patrick Moynihan, who was seen by some as a racist. Andrew Young, running for mayor of Atlanta in 1981, counseled patience in response to the black community's demands to end the murders of its children. Abernathy and Williams supported Reagan's candidacy. An entire class of black farmers, sharecroppers, and rural laborers all but disappeared, eliminating part of the social foundation on which the civil rights struggles in the Deep South a generation ago had been built. As an activist in the Amalgamated Clothing Workers Union, Coleman Young had led the creation of the fiercely independent National Negro Labor Council in the 1950s; years later, as mayor of Detroit, he forged a conservative political alliance with corporate capital at the expense of black and poor constituents. Mahwah's huge automobile plant, the site of black labor militancy, has been shut down permanently, along with hundreds of other industrial plants in the Northeast and Midwest.

Despite considerable gains, black workers in the early 1970s were largely concentrated in the lowest paid semi-skilled and unskilled sectors of the workforce. Those blacks in skilled trade union positions usually had low seniority. The recession of 1974–75, combined with a political drift to the right in national politics, greatly worsened the position of the black working class in several ways. The exporting of capital and jobs, especially by multinational corporations, reduced the number of jobs available to American workers. Capital-intensive industries, particularly auto and steel, sharply cut back the number of workers with low seniority. Despite the creation of pressure groups such as the Coalition of Black Trade Unionists, blacks still have very few top to middle-level representatives within the trade union bureaucracy. In 1977 the Supreme Court reinforced racism and sexism within unions by insisting that blacks and women prove that seniority systems were designed to "intentionally discriminate" against them. For these reasons the tenuous relationship between black progressive groups and organized labor was increasingly antagonistic, even bitter.

CRISIS OF BLACK LABOR

The acceleration of black unemployment and underemployment, the capitulation of many civil rights and Black Power leaders to the right, the demise of militant black working-class institutions and labor caucuses, and the growing dependency of broad segments of the black community upon public assistance programs and transfer payments of various kinds are not mutually exclusive phenomena. These interdependent realities are the beginnings of a new and profound crisis for black labor. As Harold Baron notes, the capitalist class historically has needed "black workers, yet the conditions of satisfying this need compel it to bring together the potential forces for the most effective opposition to its policies, and even for a threat to its very existence. Even if the capitalists were willing to forgo their economic and status gains from racial oppression, they could not do so without shaking up all of the intricate concessions and consensual arrangements through which the State now exercises legitimate authority."

Despite the destruction of de jure segregation, the white capitalist class has not abandoned racism. Instead, it has transformed its political economy in such a way as to make the historic "demand for black labor" less essential. In the production of new goods and services, from semiconductors to petroleum products, the necessity for poorly paid operatives, semiskilled laborers, and service workers becomes progressively less with advances in new technology. Simultaneously the white capitalist class has succeeded in developing a strong black political current against black participation in unions. Leading representatives of the black petit bourgeoisie are in outspoken opposition to public-sector union activities in metropolitan centers dominated by newly elected black officials.

The historic evolution of the black working class in advanced capitalism and the ambiguous relation between blacks and organized labor raise a series of difficult questions. Is there any real basis for working-class unity within the trade union movement and, more generally, within American politics? Does unionization help or hinder the economic advancement of blacks vis-à-vis whites? Are unions "structurally racist" in a race-oriented and class-dominated society, unable by virtue of their very existence to advance the material interests of black laborers?

The negative signs can be summarized in a single case, the now classic example of budding unity between black politicians and the Chamber of Commerce against black public employees in Atlanta in 1977. The consensus among black middle-class leaders, many of them civil rights veterans, held that unions were, at best, unreliable allies and perhaps even structural obstacles to black socioeconomic advancement under capitalism. Atlanta's 900 black sanitation workers, members of AFSCME, nevertheless campaigned aggressively to elect Maynard Jackson as the city's first black mayor. Under Jackson's rule, the sanitation workers averaged annual salaries of $7,500 and received no wage increases in three years. After negotiations failed, black public employees went out on strike. Jackson's immediate response—to fire the workers—won the praise alike of Atlanta's corporations, media, and the black petit bourgeoisie. AFSCME President Jerry Wurf, a progressive with a history of supporting civil rights causes, was condemned as a "racist manipulator" who sought the demise of black political power in Atlanta. The Reverend Martin Luther King, Sr., informed the press that Jackson should "fire the hell out of" strikers.

Such are the harsh realities of managerial techniques in the hands of black middle-of-the-road politicians. Unions serve as scapegoats for generations of corruption and inefficiency inherited by black officeholders, while capitalism is portrayed as democratic, even potentially egalitarian. Black think-tankers at the Lincoln and Hoover Institutes meanwhile spin doctrines that make labor organizations the prime source of racism in the job market.

Racism still exists within all unions, even those with the best records. Most white union leaders tolerate the systematic exclusion of their black members from the highest paid and most skilled positions. Yet public opinion polls and electoral results show that blacks continue to support pro-labor candidates and legislation favorable to unionization. Is this an archaism, as New Right leaders contend, a sentimental remnant of an era that hardly occurred and that now stands in some distant background?

Actually, most Afro-Americans, blue- or white-collar, service or public sector workers, comprehend that unionization has historically produced higher wages, both in absolute terms and relative to white employees with similar educational backgrounds and skills. Unionization means better working conditions and a greater likelihood of upward mobility. The ratio of nonwhite to white males median incomes for all occupations in 1970 was 83 percent in unions and 62 percent outside unions; for females, 91 versus 82 percent. A substantial body of research points to the egalitarian effects of unionization upon the dispersion of fringe benefits—most especially in capital-intensive industries where black-white cooperation has kept the union spirit alive.

The divergence in attitudes between some black middle-class leaders and the great majority of black workers on unions and bi-racial labor alliances can be explained by structural differences within the black community. Blacks with college educations and professional degrees who are employed in white-collar work as professionals, technicians, managers, and administrators uniformly experience low rates of unemployment, while the burden of black joblessness falls squarely upon the shoulders of blue-collar and service workers.

The critical irony is that Reaganite policies, which most affect the poor of all races, inherently damage the black population as a whole and endanger the very right-of-center alliance that conservatives hope to achieve with the black elite. Historically, the parallel of segregation and non-unionism in the South provides a most convincing example. The relatively recent development of food stamp, public housing, and Medicaid programs illustrates the same lesson in another way. By 1979, 35 percent of food stamp recipients were black, as were 39 percent of families in subsidized housing and 30 percent of families receiving Medicaid. At these percentages in an era of raging inflation, government programs did not bail out some hopeless sector of black indigence; rather, they kept the "working poor" in jobs, off welfare rolls, out of prison, and in the constituency of black politicians. They should have reinforced a common bond across race lines among those now threatened by the policies of the New Right.

Indeed, the chief beneficiaries of social programs, those of all races with incomes of $20,000 or less in 1982 dollars, constitute a potential majority for a left-of-center coalition. But while the cruel hoax of trickle-down economics shatters the optimistic expectations of black neoconservatives, the persistence of white racism, the mobilization of cultural conservatism and political reaction threaten to derail the necessary coalition-building.

This situation is rendered all the more dangerous by the broad shifts in the character of production. Capital is in the midst of a major crisis of accumulation. The corporate prescription for restoring profits at the expense of the working class is based increasingly upon the recognition that certain sectors must drastically reduce the number of employees in order simply to

survive. Old-line industries, including auto, steel, textiles, appliances, construction, electrical and non-electrical machinery,
food and tobacco manufactures, together employing one-third
of the workforce, once constituted the foundation for corporate
growth. But projected real growth, with "Reagan reform" allowing for accelerated depreciation allowances, will be 2 percent,
less than half the rate of return during the previous two decades.
Between 1973 and 1981 alone, twenty-three tire plants shut down;
11 percent of America's steel industry has been phased out since
1977; defense-related firms, chemical, food processing, and steel
plants continue leaving the industrial Northeast and Midwest for
the Sun Belt; in New York City alone up to 50,000 jobs in the
apparel and textile industries disappeared in the 1970s. Government employment, particularly in lower-paid white- and
blue-collar service jobs, shrinks drastically at capital's command,
while the superprofits in energy, high-tech, semi-conductor and
computer industries promise a relative handful of jobs. In general, blacks have been excluded from the very sectors that are
experiencing rapid growth. The irony is sharpest in farming,
where southern blacks long occupied a central position; just as
agribusiness experiences a boom, black agricultural workers and
owners have been pushed out, relegated to insignificance.

The prospect is stark. These economic changes, coupled with
reductions in social services and benefits—the "social wage"—
can be achieved only by intensifying long-standing divisions
among the poor and the angry. The principal tactic of the New
Right is to push cultural issues with a special appeal for white
ethnic voters and many lower-income groups, diverting attention
from economics and focusing instead on abortion, school prayer,
de facto segregation, defeat of the Equal Rights Amendment,
prevention of gay rights legislation and of all affirmative action
 statutes. In short, the New Right aims to rebuild fixed hier-
archies, ideological, sexual, class, and racial, and to abandon
those social values that unions have at their best represented. The
strength of this potential counterrevolution depends upon the
ability of the state to create allies within the very classes it is
committed to exploiting.

The common stake that unions and the black working class share should be abundantly clear. If black progressives and activists do not reevaluate their position on labor unions, even with all the obvious racist contradictions, they may alienate themselves from the black working class and participate in that class's ultimate destruction. If white union activists are not prepared to wage an uncompromising struggle against racial bigotry within the various sectors of the working class and to engage in principled dialogues with black leaders on myriad economic issues that transcend the narrow "economism" of wages and hours, workers themselves will inevitably suffer. All the historic gains of labor are endangered. Make no mistake: the organic crisis afflicting the black working class will extend to workers of all descriptions.

The vision of a more egalitarian future is no longer a cloudy distant utopia, no mere desired goal but an immediate material need. The crisis of the black working class cannot be resolved except by a multiracial program for social transformation forged in the industrial and public service unions. The great (and still unanswered) question is, Will unions (and white labor generally) overturn their own contradictory traditions, exclusionary norms, and unconscious racist ideology? The contemporary government and employer assault against labor cannot succeed if labor unites against racism and for human equality. The failure to confront the issue not only restrains our grandest hopes but may provide the foundation for the permanent conservative hegemony over once-proud unions and workers—and perhaps, at some later time, over an authoritarian or even fascist social order.

Solidarity Day march and rally, Washington, D.C., 1981. Photo courtesy of *AFL-CIO News*.

Labor and Capital Today and Tomorrow

Sidney Lens

As the 1980s opened, the public stance of labor's hierarchs was one of self-satisfaction, reminiscent of the mood of the old-line officials who surrounded William Green in the early 1930s. There was no sense of crisis. Gus Tyler, a retired official of the International Ladies Garment Workers Union and columnist for the *AFL-CIO News,* wrote a piece outlining a scenario for American expansion that would give wings to unions "as employment grows in building, construction, seafaring, capital-intensive manufacturing and teaching." Lane Kirkland, a few months after taking the AFL-CIO scepter from the ailing George Meany, castigated the "prophets of doom" for misreading "both the present strength and the future prospects of trade unionism for America." He predicted "substantial gains in union membership over the next decade," especially "in industries and geographic areas in which progress has been slow."

The assumptions here were that labor history was a continuum free from startling quantum jumps. In fact, however, the movement had reached dead ends on a number of occasions in the past, when wide-ranging changes in the character of capitalism diminished labor's strength and dictated severe modifications in program. The 1880s were such a period. The "uplift" unionism of the Knights of Labor, based on producer cooperatives and reform but opposing the use of strikes, was out of tune with thriving and arrogant industrial capitalists, who would submit only when forced by workers who shut down a rail line, a construction site, or a printing industry. The AFL went too far in the other direction from the Knights, eschewing the socialist politics of its founders in favor of "simple, bread-and-butter unionism." But in matching power with power in strikes, and by structuring itself into craft unions, the AFL better responded to the contours of capitalism in those days than did the general assemblies of the Knights, and it was able to build a movement with some muscle behind it.

The 1930s were another such period, when labor again found itself out of tune with history. The craft structure of the AFL could not be adapted to the mass-production industrial corporations—the core of capitalism by that time; nor could the "reward your friends punish your enemies" political strategy bring about the passage of unemployment compensation, welfare, social security, and labor relations laws and other reforms. Had it not been for the formation of the Congress of Industrial Organizations, with its emphasis on industrial structure and "social" (but not social-*ist*) unionism, the movement would have remained an impotent pygmy. Again, the CIO did not go as far as it might have, and the radicals who led its major strikes and organizing campaigns were in due course either moderated or replaced. But the CIO was a major advance, not only for labor but also for the country.

In the 1980s, contrary to the consoling phrases of Tyler and Kirkland, there are unmistakable signs that the movement has again reached a crisis. Kirkland boasted that, allowing for expulsion of the Teamsters and the secession of the United Auto Workers—the two largest affiliates of the AFL-CIO—the "remaining unions actually increased their membership by 3.5 million, about a third," between 1955 and 1979. Pursuing his arithmetic further, he listed a host of unions that had lost members because of changes in technology but showed how this was compensated for by gains of other unions—716,000 for state, county and municipal employees, 373,000 for teachers, 293,000 for service employees, and lesser gains for a few others. But this picture covered over the indisputable fact that labor had lost momentum and attractiveness—and, even more, that it had drastically declined in power vis-à-vis both industry and government. In the jargon of Chicago, it had lost its "clout."

AFL-CIO President Kirkland might be satisfied with the record, but his movement has far less appeal to working people (and citizens) now than it had about thirty years ago. Back in 1950, unions won 73 percent of National Labor Relations Board elections. In 8,043 representation elections conducted by the NLRB in 1979, unions won only 45 percent, a slight decline from the 50 percent of the previous decade. In the quarter-century Kirkland was talking about, the workforce had grown by more than 30 million, but less than 3 million had joined unions, and those were largely in one field: federal, state and local government. Very few new members came in from manufacturing and mining.

And these statistics tell only a small part of the story. As great a force as the United Mine Workers, once the most militant segment in the movement, now included only half the nation's coal miners and was bound to decline further as coal-digging continued to shift west of the Mississippi. The building trades, once the bastion of the AFL and later of the AFL-CIO, were in retreat under pressure from the Construction Users Business Roundtable, the Committee for a Union-Free Environment, the American Building Contractors, and other business groups that promote non-union construction. The proud printing trades unions were severely decimated by technology; the Newspaper Guild was losing ground steadily; the steel union watched helplessly as the basic steel industry contracted. And the auto workers were on the verge of a great jolt, as the "world car" threatened to shift much of the operations of GM, Ford, and Chrysler to foreign soil and slim down UAW ranks here by hundreds of thousands.

Even the Teamsters were being seriously challenged by the movement of employers south and west, and the establishment of non-union pockets by such operators as Overnite and Viking. More and more employers were demanding—and getting—"give backs" and concessions won yesterday were given up today, as management pleaded hard times. And more and more there were plant shutdowns—even of plants earning profits (U.S. Steel in Youngstown was one example) whose owners found it more profitable, because of tax benefits, to close down than to operate.

In 1979–80 the movement had to take a cut in real wages for the first time since World War II. President Carter—scoring a dubious first—decreed "voluntary" (in reality, mandatory) wage guidelines of 7 percent in 1979 and 9 percent in 1980, even though inflation was running about 5 percent higher in each of those years. "Worker buying power shrinks for 12th month," the *AFL-CIO News* screamed in banner headlines on June 28, 1980, "Real wages down 7.7 percent over year." Moreover, under the "re-industrialization" program advocated by both Carter and Reagan in the 1980 presidential elections, it was almost certain that living standards for workers would decline further. Carter's economic development advisor, Amitai Etzioni, predicted that the plan would bring ten more years of "belt-tightening." All of this was a far cry from the joyous projections of old-line union officials.

To add to such woes the movement had also lost public respect. For most Americans, including millions of union members, the union was simply another business, and not always an exemplary one. There were frequent stories of corruption among the Teamsters, of links to the Mafia, of despoilment of pension funds. The vast majority of unions, of course, were "clean" as far as racketeering was concerned. But reports of scores of leaders representing workers in the $15,000 and $20,000 a year class earning upward of $100,000 a year—even such political liberals as Jerry Wurf of AFSCME or Albert Shanker of the AFT—hardly projected an image of idealistic self-sacrifice.

Yet leaving aside labor's apparent weaknesses, including its unpleasant image, the core of the movement's problem clearly was a decline in relative power. Assuming that the unions had made small membership gains, as Kirkland insisted, they had nevertheless failed to keep pace with the immense new concentration of power in the hands of business and a business-oriented government. By the late 1970s the top hundred manufacturing corporations (out of 1.5 million) earned half of all American manufacturing profits, and the top 500 earned 80 percent. In 1955 there had been only 65 industrial companies with assets of $1 billion; by 1977 the figure was 193, and there were 26 firms with assets upward of $5 billion and 12 with assets of at least $10 billion. The "Fortune 500" industrial corporations (only a tiny fraction of 1 percent of such companies) employed 75 percent of all workers in manufacturing. The ten leading banks (out of 14,000) held more than a quarter of all bank assets, and the top 100 held half.

Not only was the concentration of capital more pronounced, but its form had also shifted. It had become immensely more *trans*-industrial and *trans*-national. By way of example, in 1961 International Telephone and Telegraph Company had $1 billion in assets and virtually all of its operations were in telecommunications. By the 1970s it had acquired a hundred subsidiaries worth four times that much, here and in seventy other countries. Only one-sixth of its investments were now in telecommunications, and it was dealing with at least fifteen major unions—auto workers, teamsters, communications workers, electrical workers, bakers, plumbers, machinists, steelworkers, hotel workers, and others. A strike at any one of its companies—say, Wonder Bread—was hardly more than an irritant, since the losses could be absorbed without much pain by other subsidiaries not on strike. And there was little danger that the many unions with interests in ITT would combine their efforts to shut down the company's total operations.

GLOBALIZATION

Corporate globalization, too, had punctuated the immense disparity in power between capital and labor. A Department of Commerce study of 298 global firms (multinationals) showed that by 1970 sales of their foreign subsidiaries amounted to 37 percent of their total sales and accounted for 44 percent of their profits. American plants, especially those in labor intensive fields, had moved wholesale to low-wage areas—Korea, Taiwan, Ghana, Hong Kong. Thus the strike weapon—labor's main instrument of defense for a century—was seriously blunted. Under the present structure there is no way for a single union to bargain for workers across the board in a conglomerate or multi-national corporation. Nor is there an effective mechanism for a dozen or more unions, here and abroad, to pool their strength against a single global corporation. Moreover, the strike weapon will be blunted further if present plans for robotization reach fruition. Harley Shaiken has noted that robots, already used extensively in welding, "can switch from one model to another with nothing more than new instructions, rather than the extensive retooling that conventional forms of production require. And as robot technology matures, its cost advantages become more impressive. A $40,000 Unimate Robot working two shifts over an eight-year period costs about $4.80 an hour, compared with the current labor cost of approximately $15 hourly for an auto assembler." And robots do not go on strike.

Labor's relative impotence is especially evident on the political front. Its record in recent years has been dolorous. It has been unable to repeal anti-labor laws such as Taft-Hartley, unable to win the right of common-situs picketing or to gain long-delayed major reforms such as national health service. Most of all, it has had painfully little influence on government decisions that affect workers' lives. In the 1930s the Roosevelt administration had shifted from the philosophy of laissez-faire to that of controlled capitalism in which government intervention in the economy was extensive. In the 1960s and 1970s government went a long step further toward state-*managed* capitalism. Government—federal, state, and local—now dispensed a third of the national income. Its decisions on money, regulation, subsidies, taxes and a hundred other matters helped shape the economy as never before. If it reduced the military budget, for instance, workers at 100,000 defense plants faced the loss of overtime or their jobs; if it decontrolled the price of gasoline, workers' living standards everywhere would be cut accordingly; if it raised interest rates through an action of the Federal Reserve Board, it would reduce the purchases of new homes and throw construction workers out of jobs. Thus, increasingly, labor's problems are political.

Taking these two broad-based historical changes into account, it was evident that a reinvigorated labor movement would have to change direction, not only to regain the militancy of the 1930s but also to pool the power of workers in conglomerates and multinational industries. The present national unions (called internationals) which operate in a single industry or craft are adequate in such fields as retail or services or government, where management does not cross industrial or national boundaries. But labor would probably have to add a worker-controlled "company" union structure to the present forms—a single union, say, for all ITT workers, no matter what industry they were in, including ITT workers abroad. In July 1958 an Allis-Chalmers Inter-Union Joint Conference was formed of delegates from the United Auto Workers, Steelworkers, International Union of Electrical Workers (IUE), International Brotherhood of Electrical Workers, Machinists, Firemen and Oilers. Each pledged to ask for the same package. But this pickup type of unity has not extended very far, in large part because the unions involved are too jealous of their prerogatives.

The center of power in the labor movement for many decades had been the city central body. Samuel Gompers changed that by grouping local unions into internationals and deliberately downgrading the power of city centrals. Now a new structure is indicated, one with autonomous power like the internationals, fashioned to meet the challenge of the conglomerates and multinationals.

Of greater significance for the future would be the shift from a unionism oriented toward economic concessions to one oriented toward political gains. That change seems to be indispensable. If American labor were to follow the British pattern, the AFL-CIO would be the central part of an alliance with antiwar, anti-nuke, civil rights, feminist, native American, environmentalist and other progressive movements. William Winpisinger, president of the Machinists (and the only top labor leader in decades who calls himself a socialist) has proposed for his organization a policy of "coalitionism" that could be the precursor to an American Labor party. "Coalitionism"—the concept of uniting with outside groups for specific objectives, such as demonstrating against the petroleum barons—is an indicated transition step toward independent labor politics.

As the 1980s opened there were few signs of impending changes in labor structure, ideology, and politics. There were few left-wing forces on the scene. The "revolutionary union movements" that had made some headway among black workers in Detroit had spent themselves. Ed Sadlowski's challenge to Lloyd McBride for the presidency of the Steelworkers in 1977 had captured the imagination of leftists around the country, even though his specific program had been moderate, centering on a basic point: union democracy. But Sadlowski's leftist politics were well known, and a victory for the young director of District 31 might have offered a rallying center for those seeking fundamental change. Another "vital impetus" might have come from the Coalition of Labor Union Women (CLUW), which was expected to speak for the 6.7 million women in the house of labor. But CLUW, though headed by a woman whose politics have been left of center, has remained too close to the hierarchy to make a difference.

The force that will spark a new labor left is not yet on the horizon as these words are written. The same could have been said of labor in 1932. But sooner or later, the demands of history bring into being human protagonists who form around those demands—as in 1886 and 1935. The 1980s are no exception.

Supplementary Reading

Avrich, Paul. *The Haymarket Tragedy.* Princeton: Princeton University Press, 1984.

Brecher, Jeremy. *Strike!* Boston: South End Press, 1977 ed.

Brody, David. *Workers in Industrial America: Essays on the Twentieth-Century Struggle.* New York: Oxford University Press, 1979.

Buhle, Mari Jo. *Women and American Socialism, 1870-1920.* Urbana: University of Illinois Press, 1981.

Buhle, Paul, ed. *Labor's Joke Book: An Historical Collection.* St. Louis: WD Press, 1985.

Dawley, Alan. *Class and Community: The Industrial Revolution in Lynn.* Cambridge: Harvard University Press, 1976.

Dublin, Thomas. *Women at Work: The Transformation of Work and Community in Lowell, Massachusetts, 1826-1860.* New York: Columbia University Press, 1979.

Dubofsky, Melvyn. *We Shall Be All: A History of the Industrial Workers of the World.* New York: Times Books, 1972.

Dye, Nancy Shrom. *As Equals and as Sisters: Feminism, the Labor Movement, and the Women's Trade Union League of New York.* Columbia: University of Missouri Press, 1980.

Epstein, Melech. *Jewish Labor in the U.S.A., 1882-1952.* Rev. ed. New York: Ktav, 1969.

Fink, Leon. *Workingmen's Democracy: The Knights of Labor and American Politics.* Urbana: University of Illinois Press, 1983.

Foner, Philip S. *History of the Labor Movement in the United States.* 5 vols. New York: International, 1947—.

___. *Women and the American Labor Movement.* 2 vols. New York: Free Press, 1979-80.

Frisch, Michael H., and Walkowitz, Daniel J., eds. *Working-Class America: Essays on Labor, Community, and American Society.* Urbana: University of Illinois Press, 1983.

Green, James R. *The World of the Worker: Labor in Twentieth-Century America.* New York: Hill & Wang, 1978.

——, ed. *Workers' Struggles, Past and Present: A "Radical America" Reader.* Philadelphia: Temple University Press, 1983.

Goodwyn, Lawrence. *The Populist Movement: A Short History of the Agrarian Revolt in America.* New York: Oxford University Press, 1978.

Gutman, Herbert G. *Work, Culture, and Society in Industrializing America.* New York: Alfred A. Knopf, 1976.

——, and Kealey, Gregory S., eds. *Many Pasts: Readings in American Social History.* 2 vols. Englewood Cliffs, N.J.: Prentice-Hall, 1973.

Janiewski, Dolores. *Sisterhood Denied: Race, Gender, and Class in a New South Community.* Philadelphia: Temple University Press, 1985.

Jenson, Joan M., and Davidson, Sue, eds. *A Needle, a Bobbin, a Strike: Women Needleworkers in America.* Philadelphia: Temple University Press, 1984.

Keeran, Roger. *The Communist Party and the Auto Workers' Unions.* Bloomington: Indiana University Press, 1980.

Keil, Hartmut, and Jentz, John B., eds. *German Workers in Industrial Chicago, 1850–1910: A Comparative Perspective.* DeKalb: Northern Illinois University Press, 1983.

Kessler-Harris, Alice. *Out to Work.* New York: Oxford University Press, 1982.

Laslett, J. H. M. *Labor and the Left.* New York: Basic Books, 1970.

Laurie, Bruce. *Working People of Philadelphia, 1800–1850.* Philadelphia: Temple University Press, 1980.

Levine, Susan. *Labor's True Woman: Carpet Weavers, Industrialization, and Labor Reform in the Gilded Age.* Philadelphia: Temple University Press, 1984.

Lipsitz, George. *Class and Culture in Cold War America: A Rainbow at Midnight.* South Hadley, Mass.: J. F. Bergin, 1981.

London, Joan, and Anderson, Henry. *So Shall Ye Reap.* New York: Apollo, 1971.

Lynd, Staughton. *The Fight against Shutdowns.* San Pedro, Cal.: Singlejack, 1983.

Meier, August, and Rudwick, Elliott. *Black Detroit and the Rise of the U.A.W.* New York: Oxford University Press, 1981.

Miller, Marc S., ed. *Working Lives: The "Southern Exposure" History of Labor in the South.* New York: Pantheon, 1981.

Montgomery, David. *Beyond Equality: Labor and the Radical Republicans, 1862-72.* Paperback ed., Urbana: University of Illinois Press, 1981.

———. *Workers' Control in America: Studies in the History of Work, Technology, and Labor Struggles.* New York: Cambridge University Press, 1980.

Morris, Richard B. *Government and Labor in Early America.* New York: Octagon, 1965.

Pessen, Edward. *Most Uncommon Jacksonians: The Radical Leaders of the Early Labor Movement.* Albany: State University of New York Press, 1967.

Rachleff, Peter. *Black Labor in the South.* Philadelphia: Temple University Press, 1984.

Salvatore, Nick. *Eugene V. Debs: Citizen and Socialist.* Urbana: University of Illinois Press, 1982.

Saxton, Alexander. *Indispensable Enemy: Labor and the Anti-Chinese Movement in California.* Berkeley: University of California Press, 1971.

Schatz, Ronald W. *The Electrical Workers: A History of Labor at General Electric and Westinghouse, 1923-60.* Urbana: University of Illinois Press, 1983.

Tax, Meredith. *The Rising of the Women.* New York: Monthly Review Press, 1981.

Weinstein, James. *The Decline of Socialism in America, 1912-25.* Paperback ed., New Brunswick: Rutgers University Press, 1984.

Wertheimer, Barbara Mayer. *We Were There: The Story of Working Women in America.* New York: Pantheon, 1975.

Wilentz, Sean. *Chants Democratic: New York City and the Rise of the American Working Class, 1788-1850.* New York: Oxford University Press, 1984.

Notes on Contributors

MARI JO BUHLE is a member of the history department at Brown University. She is the author of *Women and American Socialism, 1870-1920* and co-editor of *The Concise History of Woman Suffrage*.

PAUL BUHLE is director of the Oral History of the American Left, Tamiment Library, New York University. With Mari Jo Buhle he edited *The Concise History of Woman Suffrage*.

ALAN DAWLEY is in the history department at Trenton State College. Among his publications is *Class and Community: Industrial Revolution in Lynn*, a Bancroft Prize winner.

ERIC FONER is professor of history at Columbia University. He is the author of several books, including *Free Soil, Free Men* and *Thomas Paine*.

JAMES R. GREEN is a member of the history department at the University of Massachusetts at Boston. His most recent book is *The World of the Worker: Labor in Twentieth-Century America*.

SIDNEY LENS, contributing editor of *The Progressive*, has written many books on labor and foreign affairs. His latest is an autobiography, *Unrepentant Radical*.

GEORGE LIPSITZ is the author of *Class and Culture in Cold War America: A Rainbow at Midnight*. He is currently teaching at the University of Houston, Clear Lake City.

MANNING MARABLE is a professor of political sociology and director of the Africana and Hispanic Studies program of Colgate University.

DAVID MONTGOMERY is professor of history at Yale University and is the author of *Workers' Control in America: Studies in the History of Work, Technology, and Labor Struggles* and of *Beyond Equality: Labor and the Radical Republicans, 1862–72,* among other books.

NELL IRVIN PAINTER teaches history at the University of North Carolina and is the author of *The Exodusters* and *Hosea Hudson: The Narrative of a Black Communist in Alabama.*

FRANKLIN ROSEMONT is secretary of the Union Printers' Historical Society and a member of the board of the Illinois Labor History Society. His most recent book is *Isadora Speaks.*

RICHARD THOMAS is an associate professor in the College of Urban Development at Michigan State University.

BARBARA MAYER WERTHEIMER, a noted labor educator, was also the author of *We Were There: The Story of Working Women in America* and of *Labor Education for Women Workers.*

ALFRED YOUNG, professor of history at Northern Illinois University, is at work on a book entitled *The Craftsman as Citizen and the Shaping of a Nation.* His most recent book is *The American Revolution: Explorations in the History of American Radicalism.*